Manage
Your Financial Life

Manage
Your Financial Life

A THOUGHTFUL, ORGANIZED
APPROACH FOR WOMEN

NANCY DOYLE

ISBN 978-0-9976097-0-7

Note: The information I provide in this book is provided only as a source of information. This book and the information provided in it is not intended to be used as the basis for investment decisions, and nothing in this book should be considered a solicitation to buy any particular financial instrument or security. You have to make your own investment decisions based on your specific financial needs, goals, and risk tolerance.

Contents

Preface

JUST AS WE all have a personal life and a professional life, a social life and a family life, we all have a financial life. And, just as some people adeptly manage their personal, professional, social, and family lives, some people skillfully manage their financial lives.

Most of us, however, find juggling the various aspects of our lives challenging. We may turn to experts—people, books, online resources—for advice on how best to manage certain elements of our lives. Although articles abound on how to succeed professionally, how to be a better parent, and how to have a more rewarding social life, practical and easy-to-understand advice on running your financial life can be hard to find. It is true that a lot has been written about how to prepare a budget and how to handle debt. But managing your financial life is about more than just monitoring your expenses and using debt wisely. It is not just about sticking to a budget or making a savings plan. Managing your financial life is also about being organized, being informed, and figuring out what you do with your money—and how to invest it.

Many people want to learn about finance and investing, but they don't know how or where to start. I have yet to find a resource that offers comprehensive, objective, and helpful ways to learn how to manage one's financial life. I wrote this book in an attempt to fill that gap.

In this book, I offer a plan that you can implement to take control of your financial life. This plan is based on:

- My professional experience as a credit analyst, stock analyst, CFA® charterholder, and consultant
- My real-life experience as a wife, mother, daughter, sister, and friend
- The real-life experiences of my family and friends

The first step in this plan is to get organized. For most of us, our lives are overscheduled and time is a precious commodity. Organization is essential for managing day-to-day tasks and achieving goals. Being organized also helps you manage your finances more easily and with greater discipline. Part of being organized is implementing a system for tracking your financial information. Keeping records, whether they are paper or electronic, is more complicated in today's world than it was in the past. Most people hang onto things that don't matter much and, as a result, they often cannot find what they need when they need it. Having a system for organizing your important files and documents will help you keep less stuff and manage your finances more efficiently.

After getting organized, the next steps in the plan are to analyze your financial profile objectively, to learn about investing, and then to put it all together and invest your money. My hope is that this book will help you take an objective view of your finances, build on your understanding of finance and investing concepts, and apply that knowledge in your everyday life. What I propose here is a process, not a race. It will take some time—you don't need to take every step right away.

Throughout the book, "sidebars" and "real-life experiences" illustrate points or expand on topics. Sidebars explain concepts, industry jargon, or what a saying actually means. I also provide examples of real-life situations from my own experiences and those of family and friends.

My philosophy on finances is similar to my philosophy on life: I tend to be both conservative and optimistic. I am a forthright person who believes that simple is good. Being organized is a priority, and I strive to reduce stress in my life. And I like to sleep well. The path that I outline in this book embodies all these characteristics. You will notice a few quotes from Benjamin Franklin. Although some of the financial concepts covered may be new to you, most of the ideas and principles I touch on here have stood the test of time.

A Starting Point

In the wake of the 2008 global financial crisis, I was distressed to discover how many people did not understand the various risks associated with their financial profiles. The crisis had a profound impact not only on people's finances but also on their lives. To me, it clearly illustrated the importance of being informed and thoughtful about one's finances. It also sparked my interest in exploring how to help people manage their financial lives.

Contrary to what you might think, you do not need to have a CPA or MBA to invest your money. My mother did not have a degree in finance or accounting, but she was a successful life-long investor. I believe there are several reasons why:

- She was encouraged to learn about investing at an early age.
- She understood the importance of saving and investing.
- She enjoyed managing her finances and stayed engaged in managing them throughout her life.

. . . .

For my mother's twentieth birthday, her grandmother gave her twenty shares of stock in a company. My mother followed that company closely throughout her life and kept up with corporate news. She was confident in the company's prospects, and she never sold a share. In fact, she reinvested all her dividends back into company stock. Over the years, the stock appreciated and split seven times. When my mother died, she had been a shareholder of General Electric for fifty-five years. Those twenty shares had grown to more than ten thousand.

. . . .

Even if you have a financial background, there are plenty of opportunities to continue learning. The financial world is always evolving, and your financial needs will inevitably change as you age. I have a BA in economics and an MBA in finance. In my education and early career, I focused on corporate finance—how companies fund themselves. In the mid-1990s, I decided to pursue a career in the investment industry. Until that point, most of what I had learned about investing was from my parents and my husband. My first job in the investment industry was in a research department at an investment bank, where I analyzed financial stocks. The work was fascinating, and I was eager to learn.

A few years after landing my first job in the investment industry, I became a mom, and my life got a lot busier. Although I was licensed to buy and sell investments, I hired someone to help manage our family's money. I still use the same person I hired twenty years ago. Although I work with a financial adviser, I also make investments on my own.

An Objective Perspective

I bring an objective and straightforward perspective on managing finances. When it comes to money, I believe that independence and objectivity are crucial. Although there are plenty of impartial articles and books written by academics that address finance and investing, these can be complex and hard to follow for people who are not steeped in the field. Many articles and books about finance and investing are written by people who work for or have partnered with asset management firms, banks, insurance companies, or brokerage firms. I am concerned that their advice may not be truly objective.

My perspective is different. I am an independent consultant, and I do not work for nor am I partnered with any financial services companies. I am not selling financial products, nor am I looking to attract new clients. I have put my education and professional experience into practice in my own life, and I am sharing my knowledge and experiences in this book. Like my parents, I regard learning about finance and investments as a lifelong pursuit, and I am always looking for ways to manage my financial life better.

In this book, I do not give financial, legal, accounting, or tax advice. Rather, I share my system for managing my financial life. This system has evolved over the years—as my needs and my life have changed—and works well for me. Some parts of this system may work better for you than others—use only what works for you. I have certain opinions and let you know what they are. I use numbers in this book for illustrative purposes only—they do not reflect current market conditions.

I encourage you to visit my website at www.manageyour-financiallife.com. Please feel free to ask questions and provide feedback. I welcome them.

There are several people that I'd like to thank. Over the years, it has been a privilege to work with talented people who have taught me much about finance and investing. My family and friends are an ongoing source of inspiration and support. Many have been willing to share life experiences and professional knowledge, in turn enhancing the material in this book. My book designer, Cecile Kaufman, did an excellent job creating just the right look. I truly appreciate my editor and great friend, Deirdre Greene, who first suggested that I write this book and worked with me to make it a reality. My wonderful parents, who are with me in spirit, always encouraged me to pursue my own path. Last, I am most grateful to Bill, Brendan, and Julia. Thank you for making me laugh and cheering me on. You are everything to me.

Introduction

WE ARE INUNDATED daily—sometimes hourly—with information related to finance and investments. Whether you get your news from television, print, or online sources, financial information is everywhere. It may be an alert about a dramatic change in the Dow Jones Industrial Average or an interview about the numbers behind the monthly unemployment report. It could be a video about tax planning or an article about saving for retirement. What about all the industry jargon? What does it mean?

You also may be swamped with offers from credit card, mortgage, or insurance companies. Advertisements from investment firms are ubiquitous. Many of these firms offer not only a product but also a dream. Have you ever noticed that many ads from financial firms involve images of water? Yes, living on a lake would be pleasant, but if that is your dream, how do you get there?

How does this seemingly never-ending flow of information relate to you?

Each person's response to the flood of financial information and advertising messages varies because people's financial profiles are diverse, as are their circumstances, concerns, and goals. A twentysomething might be focused on making a living while paying off student debt. A thirty- or forty-year-old—forming a household and having children—might have a goal of buying a home and saving for her children's education. Someone in middle age might be focused on retirement. As our lives change, so do our financial concerns and goals.

The paths people take through life also vary. In our grandparents' generation, a person often spent his or her entire career at one company. There was much more certainty than today—job security, good benefits, a comfortable retirement. Today, people change jobs frequently, often take on part-time or consulting work, and sometimes start their own businesses. With greater choices and greater flexibility come greater uncertainty. Given that uncertainty, you need to make sure you have control over your financial life. But comfort with your financial life is not necessarily related to the size of your paycheck or the size of your home or what stage of life you're in.

It's Time to Contemplate Your Financial Life

Regardless of your financial circumstances, now is the time to take control of your financial life. Why? To use terms from the world of economics, micro- and macroconsiderations affect your financial life. Microfactors relate to your personal situation, whereas macrofactors relate to demographic and broader economic trends.

Life transitions (microfactors)—a new job, a new house, marriage, divorce—often lead people to take a closer look at their finances. So does systemic financial turmoil (a macrofactor), such as the dot-com bubble of 2000 or the global financial crisis of 2008. As the financial world becomes ever more interconnected, what happens in Iceland is bound to have a ripple effect on people in Indiana.

If you picked up this book, you might be at a point in your life where you realize that you need a better understanding of:

* What financial information you need to hold onto
* Where your important financial documents are located
* How your investments work
* How easily you can convert your investments to cash

Or maybe you're ready to take a longer-term view of your financial situation and want to make sure that you have enough money to achieve your financial goals. For whatever reason, you picked up this book hoping it would provide a path for you to follow to take control of your financial life.

Adopt a Family Office Approach

Using the traditional definition, a family office is an entity that organizes, coordinates, manages, and protects a wealthy family's finances. For this book, however, I use the phrase "family office" to mean a comprehensive, coordinated approach to managing your financial life. In my opinion, a family office approach should not just be for the wealthy. We should all manage our financial lives in a thoughtful, coordinated manner.

When I refer to a family office approach, I am not talking about a physical space staffed with financial professionals, but rather a comprehensive, deliberate method for handling finances. Although few people have the financial resources to justify renting office space or hiring a team of investment, legal, tax, and philanthropic advisers, you can become educated, organized, and actively involved in coordinating and managing your own financial life.

Thinking about this concept of a family office might lead you to wonder what, exactly, is a family? How do your financial decisions affect your loved ones? In my mind, and for the purpose of this book, "family" is defined as broadly as multiple generations and as narrowly as a single person who wants to be self-sufficient.

No matter how you define your family, the benefits of a family office approach are numerous. Using a family office approach, you will be more informed about your financial situation, you will have a better handle on your financial risk, you will encounter less stress in your life overall, and, ultimately, you will be more successful at managing your finances.

A Book for Women

My goal is to educate, engage, and empower you while helping you simplify your financial life. The ideas I discuss in this book apply to everyone. For many reasons, however, I am writing for women, whether in a relationship or single, with or without children.

Why do I focus on women? In recent years, I have been approached by many women undergoing challenging transitions—divorce, widowhood, a major illness, losing parents—who have decided that it is time to become more informed about investing and managing their finances. I have also spoken with women who are not in transition but are at a point in their lives where they want a better understanding of how to manage their own financial affairs.

Some people find the subject of finances and the process of investing overwhelming; others don't know where to start or whom to trust. Getting a handle on your finances likely involves a mountain of paperwork—documents, statements, forms. Although "paperwork" is increasingly moving online, the sheer volume of financial information—whether paper or electronic—can lead to stress from feeling disorganized and overwhelmed.

Traditionally, most women were not actively involved in managing family finances. Given demographic and socio-economic trends, however, women should be. More women today live alone. Between 1970 and 2017, the percentage of US households with a woman living alone increased from 11.5 percent to 15.4 percent.[1] The number of married households in the United States has declined from almost 80 percent in the 1950s to almost 50 percent today.[2] Over the same period, the percentage of women who never married has risen from 20.0 percent to 29.3 percent.[3] Women tend to outlive men and have longer retirements. A 65-year-old woman today can expect to live another 20.6 years, compared to 18.0 years for a 65-year-old man.[4] The median age women become widowed in the United States is 59.4.[5]

Women in general are becoming wealthier—in terms of the rising number of wealthy women and the expanding size of their investable assets. According to Mary Quist-Newins, the author of *Women and Money: Matters of Trust*, women represent more than 40 percent of all Americans with gross investable assets greater than $600,000; 45 percent of American millionaires are women. The number of wealthy women in the United States is growing twice as fast as the number of wealthy men.

Behavioral finance studies have shown that women investors tend to be more patient and disciplined than men and to have less risk in their portfolios. Women tend to maintain a longer-term view and are more focused on their goals. Not surprisingly, women tend to achieve better investing results than men.

A woman in my community received an MBA from the same school that I attended. She graduated with distinction thirty years before me, one of only six women in her class. (My business school class was 25 percent women.) She has had a successful career and has made a point of advising younger women to read the front page of the *Wall Street Journal* every day. It is important to keep up with national and world events, but also to be informed about the most important business and financial news of the day.

Women take on many roles throughout their lives. Women are often caregivers, and helping to manage other people's finances is one aspect of the assistance that we might provide. We often put the needs of others—whether it is our parents, our partner, or our children—before our own. We all have heard the advice that we cannot help others without taking care of our own needs first—that adage holds true financially as well as physically and emotionally.

Filling a Gap

Despite the compelling socioeconomic and demographic trends, I have yet to find comprehensive personal finance resources that I consider truly helpful to women. The articles, books, websites, and videos that I have encountered are often incomplete, too complicated, or overly simplistic. They might encourage women to invest, but they don't tell them how to do so effectively. The information that is out there can perpetuate the perception that investing and personal finance are dull topics that are difficult to understand—and who has the time?

Even people in the financial services industry are not sure how to meet the needs of women who want to be more actively involved in managing their finances. A couple of years ago, I attended a "Women in Investing" luncheon hosted by an investment firm; I was looking forward to learning new information while meeting women who shared my interests. The intelligent, accomplished speaker discussed sexism and the challenges of being the wife of a politician. Although she was impressive and quite entertaining, I left the event thinking that it was a missed opportunity for the attendees to learn more about an incredibly important topic.

This book aims to fill the gap by covering important investment and financial topics and by presenting a strategy for taking control of your financial life.

A Comprehensive, Coordinated Method

Your financial decisions affect many areas of your life. This book presents a comprehensive, coordinated method for taking control of your financial life. This approach encompasses the participation of your family, however you define family, and your partner, if you have one, in managing your finances. Money can be a major source of stress in relationships, and you and your partner need to be on the same page with respect to your family's financial life.

Working together can help reduce stress around managing your finances. If you set a family meeting time (e.g., the first Sunday of the month) to discuss finances, you will more likely stick to your plans. People tend to make better decisions about savings and investments after discussing their ideas with others, especially people with diverse viewpoints. Make sure to include your partner on the journey you are about to embark on.

A Hybrid Discussion

Some authors have written extensively about debt reduction and managing day-to-day finances but little about investing.

Others have written about how to organize your life but have not focused on finance and investments.

This book presents a hybrid discussion about managing your financial life by combining education with organization. Both are integral to the process. There are four main steps to my plan: (1) get organized, (2) analyze your financial profile, (3) educate yourself about investing, and (4) invest your money.

Why is organization the first step? Search the Internet for books on organization, and you will get hundreds of pages of results with advice on everything from how to organize your pantry to how to organize your email inbox. Organizing your financial life might take more effort than organizing some other areas of your life, but the rewards can be enormous.

Being disorganized about your finances will have a profound impact on many areas of your life. When your financial life is disorganized, you might not understand what resources you have, what resources you don't have, and where your important financial information is. You will make uninformed decisions and you won't understand the riskiness of your financial profile. Your money might not be working for you or might even be working against you. Bad decisions resulting from being disorganized could result in missed opportunities, penalties, and extra taxes.

Once you've organized your financial affairs, it will be time to analyze your financial profile and assess potential risks: this is the focus of part 2. The third part of the book explains financial concepts and different ways to invest. This section is not intended to be a definitive explanation of these topics, and throughout the book I provide suggestions on other resources to consult. Finally, it will be time to put your knowledge to work, examine your goals, and invest your money, which is the subject of part 4.

Managing your financial affairs is not something that you should ignore or postpone. Just like taking care of your health and maintaining your home, you should be actively engaged in your financial life, whether you manage your own money or you use a financial adviser. Don't be passive or shy: read, ask questions, ask more questions, and seek answers. The people who are paid to provide you with financial products or help you manage your finances are also paid to answer your questions. Read periodicals like the *Wall Street Journal* regularly. The Internet has many information sources. If you use an adviser, you will be a better client if you are well informed. Even with an adviser, you cannot completely outsource, or offload, the management of your personal finances. Managing your financial life is an ongoing activity, just like maintaining a healthy work–personal life balance and a fulfilling social life.

Some Financial Truths

As you start down the path to gaining control of your financial life, there are some themes to keep in mind.

Everything Is Related

All your financial decisions are interrelated. A spending decision you make this afternoon will affect how much you can save this month. Selling a stock today will affect the taxes you will owe next April. Opening a credit card this weekend will affect the rate on a new car loan you take out next summer. Pay attention to details.

Retirement Looms No Matter Your Age

It is an unfortunate reality that the vast majority of people have not saved enough money for their retirement. The old savings model for retirement involved defined benefit plan pensions, or traditional pensions, and Social Security. Under the old model, your employer took care of investing your pension, and the government was responsible for your Social Security benefits.

In today's model, the vast majority of individuals do not have traditional defined benefit pensions. The primary source of retirement income comes from 401(k) plans, 403(b) plans, and individual retirement accounts. For those of us who are at the tail end of the baby boom or are Gen Xers, Social Security will likely look different as we enter retirement than it did for our parents. Traditional sources of retirement funds need to be supplemented by other personal investments. Because you, not your employer, are responsible for your retirement, managing your money for today and tomorrow is a task that you cannot take lightly.

Parents usually put kids' needs before their own. Most parents want to help their kids pay for school and get started in life. Many students today leave college with substantial debt, which means they put off such milestones as buying homes or having children. Some parents borrow from their retirement plans to help pay their children's tuition or to contribute to a child's down payment. The desire to help your kids is innate, but you must make retirement a priority even if you have children. If you don't ramp up your saving and investing now—no matter what life stage you are in—you risk not having enough money to retire when the time comes and, if you do have children, you may end up depending on your children for financial support later in life.

Managing Your Finances Should Be a Lifelong Pursuit

Saving and investing should be lifelong pursuits, and you are never too young to start. Your financial habits, opinions, and practices can set an example for your own children and provide them with valuable lessons. Get your kids involved at an early age. Even when they are little, children need firsthand experience with money.

Rather than give us a small cash allowance, my father kept a ledger. Each week, he would enter our allowance in the ledger, and we watched the balance grow on paper. When we wanted money for something, he would give it to us and deduct the amount from the balance in the ledger. Even for small things, like a candy bar, Dad was "the bank." Seeing the reduced balance made us think about if we really wanted or needed an item. When we had accumulated a certain amount, he took us to the bank to open saving accounts. For me, that was in 1973, when I was nine years old. I still have my first passbook.

Today, instead of using a ledger, you can use an app to track your children's allowance and be "the bank."

The teenage years are especially important for developing healthy financial habits. With their first job, kids can start to really understand the value of money. They will also encounter the impact of taxes. I still remember my first paycheck—both the thrill and the disappointment. With debit cards, teens can monitor their spending activity and understand exactly where their money goes. They will make mistakes, but these mistakes will provide opportunities to learn.

My grandfather gave us each a few shares of stock in the company where he worked. We learned how to look up the stock, or ticker, symbol in the paper. Our dividend checks were tiny, but we were thrilled when they arrived in the mail. We put the checks directly into our savings accounts. Thus even at a young age, we saw how our savings could grow. It made an impression on us.

You can pass on more lessons to your kids as they enter the working world. Help them understand the importance of saving and investing—essential habits that are best established early. Encourage them to start saving for retirement through their employer and to take advantage of corporate matches. Remind them that it is easier to put money away when they are single than it will be when they have a family to take care of. They need to understand the impact of inflation on their money and the problems that debt can create. They should think about giving back.

Some of the most successful, well-respected investors in the world are in their seventies, eighties, or older. Many have accumulated significant wealth yet keep working because they enjoy what they are doing. Investing keeps them engaged. Lifelong investors don't stop reading the *Wall Street Journal* just because they have turned eighty.

A Few More Points

Managing your financial life is a comprehensive topic. In this book, I cover a lot of ground. As you progress through the book and toward your goal of managing your financial life better, remember these ideas, or truths:

- The importance of time: Compounding is powerful.
- The importance of risk and return: There are many types of risk.
- The importance of discipline and conviction: Stay true to your plan.
- The importance of patience: Study your investment decisions and don't rush.
- The importance of value: Value is not what you paid for something. It is what someone else is willing to pay for it.
- The importance of supply and demand: Both have an impact on value.
- The importance of expectations: They also drive value.
- The importance of liquidity: How easily something can be converted to cash is key.

- The importance of total return: Look at both appreciation and income.
- The importance of taxes: Timing and keeping good records are essential.
- The importance of fees: They can really add up, especially over time.
- The importance of inflation: It affects your future spending.
- The importance of people: The person managing your money, the person managing the fund that you have invested in, and the person managing the company that you invested in all matter.

As you start this book and the journey it represents, be honest about your finances. Try to look at your financial picture the same way an objective outsider would. How risky is your profile? What are your opportunities to grow assets? Are you on track to meet your goals? Learn from your mistakes. Look at what did not turn out well in the past, figure out why, learn from it, and move on.

Being disciplined and informed regarding your financial affairs will allow you to "live a little." Don't forget the occasional splurge. Focus on one or two things that bring you joy. Saving for retirement should be a primary long-term goal, but don't forget to plan also for things that bring you happiness in the short run. This is the fun side of savings and investment—part of the emotional payoff.

It's time to get started!

PART 1

Get Organized

A place for everything, everything in its place.

—BENJAMIN FRANKLIN

Managing your financial life means managing a lot of information. In your day-to-day life, having a sense of order reduces stress and allows you to enjoy life more. When life throws you a curveball, however, being organized takes on even greater importance. This section addresses organizing your financial life—how to go through the piles of information you have sitting around and assess what information to keep and how to keep it.

CHAPTER 1

Spring-Cleaning

FIRST THINGS FIRST: it is time for a financial spring-cleaning. Just like when you go through your closet or food pantry to determine what to keep, what to donate, and what to toss, you need to do the same with your financial life

But instead of emptying your clothes closet and tossing everything on the bedroom floor, you will gather all papers and online documents related to your financial life. You will pull together and sift through information and all essential legal documents about your bank accounts, investments, insurance policies, and loans; your home; and your car(s). This can feel like an overwhelming task, but if you break it down into steps, you'll see that organizing your financial life is manageable, and the satisfaction you get once you're done will be immense.

Step 1: Assemble the Tools for the Task

If you are a paper person, set aside a room or an area of a room to work in so you can take breaks without the papers encroaching on the rest of your life. If you're an online person, keep a log of what you've dealt with as you make progress. Most of us have both paper and electronic documents to organize.

Have bins for recycling and for shredding nearby, as well as a staple remover, sticky notes, pencils, paper clips, and file folders. I also recommend that you work in uninterrupted blocks of time. This process can be tedious and even a little emotional, so make sure you give yourself some breaks.

Step 2: Gather Your Information

What kind of information am I talking about here? Most of us have a place—or a few places—in our home where we gather and keep "stuff that is important." Over time, we add boxes, files, and piles to the "stuff that is important." Soon we cannot locate what we need amid the "stuff that is important." You may not remember why you kept that receipt from the corner market or the contract from ten years ago. Moreover, you may need to locate vital information in a hurry and end up wasting a significant amount of time trying to find that information or being unable to find it at all.

My former college roommate stored "stuff that is important" in a variety of places. When she started her financial spring-cleaning, she found some passports in a desk drawer with her marriage certificate; a safe deposit box key in the drawer of her spare room's desk; information about retirement accounts in a file cabinet; bank statements in a bookcase; and documents in a safe deposit box that she'd forgotten she had.

In addition to all your "stuff that is important" boxes, files, and piles, go through your home and gather any and all documents and papers relating to financial, tax, and legal matters, including things such as:

- Bank, financial, and credit card accounts
- Insurance
- Mortgage, car loans, and student loans
- Tax returns
- Birth certificates and marriage certificates
- Wills, trusts, and powers of attorney

Gather all medical and school documents for you, your spouse, and your kids. Also gather any information related to your home and major purchases.

As you start your financial spring-cleaning, you may be surprised to find warranties and receipts for items you no longer have, repair bills for cars you no longer own, and statements from investments that you sold long ago. At the same time, sorting through papers can bring positive surprises. I know of two families who discovered life insurance policies among their late parents' papers. I also have friends and family who discovered keepsakes, such as cherished photographs and even love letters, tucked in with the financial statements.

Step 3: Determine What to Keep and What to Toss

Now that you have gathered, it is time to sort. A fundamental step in a financial spring-cleaning is determining where essential information is right now, where you should keep it, what to toss or recycle, and what to shred. This is also a great time to organize your contact and account information. Here are some general guidelines that I follow:

- Keep tax returns and all supporting documents for seven years after the filing date.

- Keep all bank statements and credit card annual statements and summaries for seven years.
- Keep a record of the purchase for every new investment, or the confirmation, for as long as you hold the investment. This documentation provides the original cost, or original **cost basis**.
- Keep year-end statements for each investment account as long as you own investments in that account. If you transfer investments to a new account at a different firm, you will need the cost basis information.
- Shred monthly statements once you receive year-end summaries for your investment accounts.
- Keep receipts for any major purchases and for all things that are insured as long as you have the item.
- Keep all records related to a home purchase and sale and any improvements that affect the home's cost basis, or the original price of the home plus the cost of modifications that enhance the home's value, indefinitely.
- Keep mortgage agreements (including payoff notices), car loan documents (and payoff notices), and documentation for any other loans indefinitely.
- Shred anything with identifying information that you no longer need. I keep both a recycle bin and a shredding bin in my office.

You may be surprised at the amount of paper that you recycle or shred. During a recent spring-cleaning, I had so many documents to shred that I decided to use a professional shredder. Professional shredding is both secure—you watch professionals put your documents in a massive shredding machine—and green—everything gets recycled. Moreover, it is not expensive and it can be a huge time-saver.

Step 4: Implement a System for Keeping Track of Information

Whether appearing in your in-box or in your mailbox, information inundates you daily, adding to the papers (virtual or real) you already have. Some of it is important; some of it is not. Not only should you strive to reduce the amount of paper and computer files that you retain, but you need a system for organizing information that you decide to keep.

Thus the next step in your financial spring-cleaning is to develop a system for keeping track of your financial life. The system you use must work for you and be one that you can easily maintain—otherwise this step will be a waste of time. Although my focus in this book is on finances, organizing your nonfinancial papers and files as well as your financial information will simplify your life overall. Examples of nonfinancial papers are documents related to your children, health care, travel, holidays, family history, and emergency contacts.

Your system can incorporate paper file folders or electronic files. Preferably, your system uses both. I use the terms "folder" and "file" interchangeably in this book. Whether you are using a paper or an electronic system, make sure that your information is secure. Password-protect computer files, especially those relating to your financial affairs. Store vital papers, such as birth certificates, wills, Social Security cards, and passports, in a fire-safe box at home or a safety deposit box at your bank.

Regardless of whether your filing system is paper or electronic, there are two main file categories: financial files and nonfinancial files. For your financial files, make a separate folder for each of the following:

- Current year taxes
- Bank accounts

- Investments (one folder for each investment or account)
- Health insurance (for the policy and to track claims)
- Other insurance policies (a separate folder for home and auto, life, and disability)
- House (for maintenance provider contacts and for receipts or invoices from renovations or significant repairs)
- Cars
- Big-ticket items (receipts for appliances, jewelry, or art and any appraisals or notes about inherited items)

As a working mom, I also rely on a folder system for my non-financial life. These files include:

- My kids' schools (one folder for each child)
- My kids' activities (program schedules and information, waivers, and so on)
- Health forms (extra copies of physical forms for camp, sports, and so on)
- Trips (upcoming travel and a file for trips that we have taken as a reference)
- Gifts (what I give each year to family members—to avoid repeats—and for my hair dresser, manicurist, dog groomer, mail carrier, and refuse and recycling collectors)
- Family history (news articles, obituaries, programs from weddings and memorial services, notes on family lore, genealogy)

Step 5: Consider Some Related Topics

As you embark on your financial spring-cleaning, this is the perfect time to focus on four subjects—passwords, taxes, beneficiaries, and going paperless.

Passwords

Time to confess: I have far too many passwords (financial accounts, online shopping, subscriptions, kids' schools, activities . . . the list goes on). I have wasted a lot of time trying to find or remember them all, and I worry about online security. Your passwords need to be secure, whether you write them on a piece of paper (keep the list hidden far from your computer) or you use a password management service.

I recently started using a password management service, which is making my life much easier. With a password management service, you store your passwords securely online. You need to remember only one master password. Once you have entered your various passwords into the service's website, you use the master password rather than entering your log-in and password for each website you visit. The password management services will alert you if your various passwords are weak and should be revised.

Taxes

Keep taxes in mind as you organize your financial life. Whether you do your own tax prep or hire a preparer or accountant, you need to keep good records. Most investments provide 1099s and other year-end tax documentation. A 1099 is a statement detailing the amount of dividends, interest, and capital gains earned during the year. Some investments are structured as partnerships and provide a year-end, or annual, K-1 instead of a 1099. A K-1 shows an investor's share of partnership income for a given year. Keep all investment documentation relating to the present year in the current tax year file. Keep all other details, such as the record of the initial investment and anything that affects the cost basis, in an investment file. The cost basis is the initial amount of the investment plus anything that affects the original cost, such as stock splits or reinvesting dividends. This kind of information is necessary for tax reporting after you sell an investment.

I keep track of this year's donations and the acknowledgments, thank you letters, and thank you emails, in the current year tax file. When I make a donation, I note the date, amount, and check number (if I wrote a check) on the solicitation letter or a printout of the email and put it in my tax file. This makes it easier to recall donations at tax time. The current IRS rule is that you need to provide an official acknowledgment for donations of $250 or more. When I receive an acknowledgment, it goes directly in the current year tax file. For more information on rules regarding donations, visit www. irs.gov/Charities-&-Non-Profits/Charitable-Organizations/ Charitable-Contributions-Written-Acknowledgments.

Beneficiary Designation

Review your beneficiaries for all insurance, investment, and retirement accounts. It is good practice to review your beneficiary designations periodically, because "life happens" and things change. Make sure your beneficiary designations are consistent with your will. Outdated beneficiary designations and inconsistencies can cause big problems.

My neighbor's sibling, a divorced parent, died without leaving a will. It was very difficult for my neighbor to access to her sibling's accounts, some of the beneficiary designations were not up to date, and my neighbor did not know her sibling's wishes. As a result, assets intended for the children went to an ex-spouse. Not only was the situation unfortunate for the children, it was a challenging situation for my neighbor.

Going Paperless

Consider signing up for paperless statements. Not only are paperless statements an environmentally friendly option, you won't have to open envelopes, file the statements, and eventually shred the statements.

Out of the mailbox, however, does not mean out of mind. Check online banking, brokerage, mutual fund, and retirement account statements regularly. It is important to keep track of the performance of your accounts and to keep an eye out for unusual activity. Most people check their online banking accounts frequently because they pay bills online. Make sure to check your brokerage, mutual fund, and retirement account statements at least quarterly.

For your online accounts, never provide a financial services company more information than necessary. For example, some financial firms give you the opportunity to aggregate account information from other firms on their site in order to generate a more comprehensive view of your financial profile. Don't do it. I am concerned about the security of displaying all your financial accounts on someone else's site. Financial firms want to know as much about you as possible for marketing purposes. It is much safer to aggregate and analyze your financial profile offline. This topic is covered in more detail in part 2.

Note which of your monthly bills are on automatic pay. If you use a credit card for some automatic payments, consider having two credit cards and devoting one to automatic payments. After you set up the automatic payments, keep the card devoted to autopay in a safe place at home. This way, if your wallet is lost or stolen, you won't have to reset all your automatic payments.

CHAPTER 2

In Case of Emergency, or ICE

*Y*OUR FINANCIAL spring-cleaning is an excellent time for "in case of emergency," or ICE, preparation.

Emergency contacts are a familiar concept. You might have emergency contact info posted in your kitchen. If you have kids, you're probably accustomed to the back-to-school ritual of filling out forms listing emergency contacts. With mobile technology, however, you can take the idea of emergency contacts a step further. If you put emergency contact info in your phone under the heading "ICE," first responders and medical personnel will know quickly whom to contact in case of an emergency.

People often forget that a key aspect of emergency contact info is letting people know where the information is located. The same is true for your finances. If there is an emergency, someone may need to step in to pay your bills or get access to cash on your behalf. Emergency situations are challenging enough. Having access to key contacts and financial accounts can help alleviate some of the stress.

My friend was very ill and went into a coma. Because his family
had all their important documents, such as power of attorney, in
one place—a binder on the bookshelf, and everyone in the household knew where and what that was—his wife was able to get the
disability process started quickly.

Step 1: Create an ICE File

An ICE—in case of emergency—file contains important documents that are easily accessible to you or to someone acting
on your behalf. There are several items to include in an ICE file:

* Essential legal documents, such as wills, powers
  of attorney (financial and health care), health care
  directives, and the titles for your home and car
* Vital records, such as birth certificates, death certificates, adoption documents, marriage certificates, military
  records, Social Security cards, and divorce documents
* Copies of passports, credit cards, and driver's licenses (it
  is prudent to keep a copy of these documents at home
  when you travel)

After you have gathered your vital documents, you need to
put them in a safe place. Having vital documents in one location makes it easier for key people to find things in an emergency. I recommend a fire-safe box if you keep documents at
home or a safety deposit box if you prefer to keep them at your
bank. Of the two options, the fire-safe box at home is more con-
venient, but the safety deposit box at the bank is more secure.
Keeping vital documents in a fire-safe or safety deposit box will
also help protect your information in case of a fire or flood.

Step 2: Formulate an ICE Plan

Whereas the ICE file includes the important documents, an
ICE plan (table 2.1) provides instructions so someone can act

on your behalf and according to your wishes. There are several steps involved in formulating an ICE plan:

1. List the name and phone number for the following people: lawyer, banker, insurance agent, accountant, investment adviser.

2. Prepare a list of bank accounts, brokerage accounts, and all other investments. Note the best sources of immediate cash, whether it is from a checking, money market, or savings account.

3. Provide details about your mortgage—the name of your mortgage company and your mortgage broker and whether payments are automatically paid from your bank account.

4. Note bills that are on automatic pay, and provide passwords or the master password if you use a password management service.

5. Inform key people of the location of the ICE file. Key people include your partner, the person who has your power of attorney, and the person designated as the executor of your estate.

6. Share your email password and other main passwords with a key person or people. Using a password management service simplifies this process because you provide the key people with a single master password. Gaining access to someone's online accounts can be extremely difficult because of strict privacy laws.

Although an ICE plan allows someone to have access to important financial and legal information in case of an emergency, there are other important considerations when someone in your family dies, such as a spouse or parent. Family members should always consult a lawyer before making any financial decisions in the wake of such a death. It is also helpful to have a few copies of the death certificate, especially for settling the deceased's affairs.

Creating an ICE plan and having discussions with key people about your wishes is effective only if you do it *before* an emergency occurs. It is good practice to review your ICE file and ICE plan periodically to make sure that it is up to date. Remember, "life happens" and things change.

Developing a system to organize your financial life for the everyday and for the unexpected is a significant accomplishment. Now you are ready to take an objective look at your finances. Analyzing your financial profile is an important step toward taking a more active role in managing your financial life.

TABLE 2.1. Sample ICE plan.

Important account Information

Company	Account Name	Account Number	Notes
First National Bank	Joint account	xxxxxx2209	Family account
Online brokerage	IRA partner 1	xxxx-6147	Roth conversion
	IRA partner 2	xxxx-5534	Roth conversion
Asset management 1	Plan sponsor XYZ Corp.	xxxx-xxxx-2345	Partner 1 401(k)
Asset management 2	Plan sponsor ABC Corp.	xxxx-xxxxxx-818	Partner 2 401(k)
Financial adviser	Joint account	xxxxxx-1863	Taxable
Mutual fund	Partner 1	xxxxx-7216	Taxable
Commodity fund	Partner 2	xxxxx-5586	Taxable
Credit cards	Card 1	xxxx-xxxx-xxxx-4216	Automatic bill pay
	Card 2	xxxx-xxxx-xxxx-8937	All other

TABLE 2.1. Sample ICE plan*(continued)*.

Key contact people

	Contact	Notes
Lawyer	John Doe (phone number)	Copy of will in the safety deposit box and John Doe's office
Accountant	Jane Smith (phone number)	Joint return
First National Bank Safety deposit box	Bob Anderson (phone number)	Downtown branch One set of keys in office desk, one in fire-safe box
Insurance agent	Bob Jones (phone number)	Jones Insurance Agency
Insurance carrier	Insurance company 1	Home and auto
Insurance carrier	Insurance company 2	Term life and disability
Mortgage broker Mortgage company	Mary Johnson (contact info.) First Mortgage Company	Mortgage documents in safety deposit box
Wilson Financial Advisers	Ed Wilson (contact info.)	Downtown location
Access to passwords	Anne Martin	Has log-in information for password management service
Bills on auto pay: Electric Gas Water Homeowner's assn.		Using automatic bill pay with credit card 1
Online payments for the following bills: Mortgage Student loan payment Credit card 1 Credit card 2		First National Bank's website

Analyze Your Financial Profile

The best way to analyze your financial profile is to use the same method that a banker would to evaluate a company for a loan or an investor would use to consider a potential investment. There are two main steps in this analysis. First, evaluate your personal financial statements to gauge your financial health. Then, consider risks to your financial profile.

Before you begin, there are three tools that I recommend you have. First, you need a calculator. A financial calculator can be helpful, but a regular calculator will suffice.

Second, I recommend picking up a financial dictionary, such as Barron's Business Guides Dictionary of Finance and Investment Terms. *You need an independent and credible source to consult as you come across terms that are unfamiliar to you.*

Third, use Excel or another spreadsheet program. Using a spreadsheet for calculations is easier than adding figures manually. In addition, most financial firms allow customers to download account information directly into Excel, which enables you to analyze and sort information without having to input all the numbers. Excel has online tutorials if you are new to the software.

Now it is time to take a look at your financial profile.

CHAPTER 3

Your Personal Financial Statements

*W*HEN EVALUATING a company, bankers and investors rely on three types of financial statements:

- An income statement, which incorporates income and expenses for a period of time
- A balance sheet, which shows net worth at a point in time
- A cash flow statement, which considers not only income but also fluctuations in savings and debt

Before you can analyze your financial profile, you need to develop your personal financial statements. I recommend starting with your income statement and then moving on to your balance sheet. After that, you can evaluate your cash flow.

Step 1: Create an Income Statement

To develop an income statement (table 3.1), start with your after-tax take-home pay. Add any other sources of income from consulting or part-time work and rental or investment income (all on an after-tax basis). If you have a partner, add your partner's after-tax take-home pay as well as any other sources of income.

TABLE 3.1. Personal income statement.		
Income		
Partner 1 take-home pay after taxes		$40,000
Partner 2 take-home pay after taxes		$48,000
		$88,000
Expenses	Monthly	Annual
Fixed		
Mortgage, taxes, etc.	$1,400	$16,800
Insurance (home, auto, term, disability)		$5,900
Car payment	$350	$4,200
Parking	$175	$2,100
Utilities	$250	$3,000
Cable, cell, etc.	$250	$3,000
Student loan payment	$775	$9,300
		$44,300
Variable		
Food and gas	$850	$10,200
Clothing and home items	$500	$6,000
Leisure	$400	$4,800
Activities	$200	$2,400
Donations	$100	$1,200
All other	$800	$9,600
		$34,200
Total expenses		$78,500
Net income		$9,500

After you add up your sources of income, subtract your expenses or obligations. Many regular, or recurring, obligations are fixed, or the same amount, every month. The main fixed recurring obligations are usually associated with your home and include your mortgage or rent; homeowners association, or HOA, fees; and real estate taxes. Other fixed recurring obligations are utilities—cable, phone, cell, electric, gas, and water bills (car and student loan payments, gym memberships). Parking may be a fixed recurring obligation.

You also incur a number of variable expenses each month. Although the amounts may vary, these expenses occur regularly and include groceries, clothing, leisure activities, children's activities (sports, music lessons, classes, camps), donations, and other miscellaneous expenses.

Your income minus your expenses equals your **net income**. To increase your net income, you have to earn more than you currently do—ask for a raise, work more hours, take on additional part-time work—or you have to reduce your current expenses. Adjusting your expenses is often the easier way to increase your net income.

I know a couple who made a decision to downsize and move to a smaller house. They chose this path not because they had become "empty nesters" or had run into financial difficulties, but because they both worked in industries where the pay was quite variable. Lowering their monthly housing expenses reduced the stress on their family budget and in their lives.

As you develop your personal income statement, take the following points into consideration.

Your Day-to-Day Expenses

For some people, personal financial management begins and ends with a budget. These people live within a strict budget with guidelines as to what to spend in various areas.

As an alternative to living on a strict budget, consider tracking all your expenses for a period of time. Monitoring your expenses is a worthwhile exercise that can help you identify ways to improve your net income.

Some diet gurus urge you write down everything that you eat when you are trying to lose weight. Keeping track of everything that you eat, even for a short period, highlights bad eating habits. The same is true for spending.

Look closely at what you spend money on and how much you spend over the course of, say, a month. Even if you do this for only a week or two, this exercise will give you a very good idea of where your money is going. You will likely discover that you are spending more on certain things than you realized. Eating out regularly, your daily latte, and your kids' activities can really add up. Look at your credit card statement and analyze your check register to categorize your spending. If you have online bank and credit card statements, export your check register and credit card information into an Excel spreadsheet. Using one credit card for everyday expenses and a different one for automatic bill payments makes this exercise much easier.

Timing of Expenses

As part of your analysis, note the timing of big expenses. Some expenses are monthly, such as mortgage payments and utilities, and some are recurring but annual or semiannual, such as tuition and insurance premiums. Some expenses, such as replacing appliances and minor car repairs, are unplanned but expected. And of course some expenses are both unplanned and unexpected. For example, there is no way to predict expenses related to home repairs following a storm. Having a cash reserve is essential if you want to be prepared for unexpected situations.

Unexpected Outflows and Inflows

Not all uncertainty leads to a negative outcome. An unexpected event could be positive. You might accept an exciting new job in an area without mass transit. This means that it is time to buy a car. In this case, buying a car entails an unexpected out-flow, but it is for a good reason. You could also have an unex-pected inflow, such as receiving a larger-than-anticipated tax refund or winning a cash prize in a charity raffle.

Unclaimed Property—An Unexpected Inflow

Each state keeps track of unclaimed property for residents. The amount of unclaimed property—utility deposits and re-funds, unclaimed paychecks, abandoned safety deposit box-es—is surprisingly large. In some states, amounts are in the billions of dollars. Check your state treasurer's website to see if you are owed anything. You never know. . . .

Step 2: Prepare a Balance Sheet

After you develop your personal income statement, it is time to look at what you are worth. The term **net worth** is frequently used to describe wealth, but its meaning is broader than that. A personal balance sheet will help you understand your net worth and, more important, what causes your net worth to fluctuate. A balance sheet clearly shows the impact that con-sumption and saving have on your financial well-being. Your net worth does not depend only on what you earn (income) or on what you have (assets); it also depends on whether you spend more or less than you earn (savings and debt).

Assets minus liabilities equals net worth. Keep this formula in mind as you think about your net worth. Table 3.2 illustrates the relationship among assets, liabilities, and net worth on a balance sheet.

A balance sheet by definition must balance. If your assets are greater than your liabilities, your net worth is positive. If your

TABLE 3.2. Personal balance sheet.

Assets		Liabilities and Net Worth	
Investable assets		Secured debts	
Checking and money market	$5,000	Mortgage	$220,000
Taxable investments	$58,000	Car loan	$15,000
Retirement assets	$75,000		
College savings	$17,000	Unsecured debts	
		Student loans	$40,000
		Credit cards	$5,000
Other assets		Total liabilities	$280,000
House	$280,000		
Car	$20,000	Net worth	$175,000
Total assets	$455,000	Total liabilities and net worth	$455,000

liabilities are greater than your assets, your net worth is negative. If you increase consumption relative to income, your debts could grow and your net worth will decline. Your income may be high enough to cover additional consumption, but you will not be saving as much as you could. In contrast, if you decrease consumption relative to income, your net worth will increase as you reduce debt or save more. The relationship among income, consumption, and net worth is covered in greater detail in the discussion of cash flow under step 3.

There are several categories on a personal balance sheet. Different categories of assets are called **asset classes**. The main types of asset classes that I focus on here are **investable assets**, which include cash and money market funds, US stocks, US bonds (corporate, or issued by companies; municipal, or issued by state or local governments; and federal, or issued by the US government), international stocks, international bonds, commodities, and currencies. You may also hear stocks and bonds referred to as **securities**. (In part 3 of this book, we will take a closer look at the various types of investments and types of investment accounts.)

As you gather information about your assets and prepare your balance sheet, build an asset allocation grid (table 3.3). An asset allocation grid is a table that aggregates your investable assets and highlights how much money you have in each asset class. Look at your financial accounts—bank, investment, retirement, and college savings—and note how much you have in each type of asset class. This is called your **current asset allocation**. Using the asset allocation in each financial account, create a grid. Total the amount in each asset class at the bottom of the grid. Total the amount in each investment account on the side.

As you create your grid, consider the **liquidity** of your assets, or how easily they can be sold or converted to cash. Liquidity is relative. Some asset classes are more liquid than others. Cash or money market funds are the most liquid assets. Stocks and bonds are fairly liquid. Retirement accounts and college savings plans may hold liquid investable assets, but the accounts have withdrawal restrictions and penalties and are therefore less liquid. With some investments, such as venture capital and private equity, your money is locked up for several years. On your asset allocation grid, put the most liquid accounts (checking and savings accounts) at the top and the least liquid accounts (retirement and college savings plans) at the bottom.

Okay, back to the balance sheet. The second category on your personal balance sheet is **other assets**. These include your home, a vacation home or investment property, car(s), and other valuable items, such as jewelry, antiques, or art. Remember to keep appraisals and receipts for these items in the appropriate folders. Also, keep notes on any special sentimental aspects of inherited objects. These notes will be appreciated by future generations.

Assets, regardless of the type, appear on the left side of the balance sheet. **Liabilities**, or debts, are listed on the right side of

TABLE 3.3. Asset allocation grid as of January X, XXXX.

	Cash/money market	Municipal bonds	Corporate bonds	Domestic stocks	International stocks
Checking account	$5,000				
Taxable investments					
Joint brokerage account	$10,000	$5,000		$12,000	
Mutual funds	$20,000		$6,000	$5,000	
College savings					
Child 1 529			$1,000	$5,500	$2,500
Child 2 529			$1,000	$4,000	$3,000
Retirement accounts					
Partner 1 401(k)			$2,500	$7,000	$3,000
Partner 2 401(k)			$3,500	$7,500	$3,000
Partner 1 IRA			$5,500	$11,500	$7,000
Partner 2 IRA			$6,000	$11,000	$7,500
Total investable assets	$35,000	$5,000	$25,500	$63,500	$26,000
% of total assets	23%	3%	16%	41%	17%
Investable assets					
By type:					
Taxable	$63,000	41%			
Retirement	$75,000	48%			
College	$17,000	11%			
Total investable assets	$155,000	100%			

the balance sheet. As with assets, there are many types of liabilities. Debt is a complicated and often confusing topic. Not understanding how debt works can lead to costly mistakes. In addition to referring to your dictionary of finance and investment terms, you might want to visit the Consumer Financial Protection Bureau at www.consumerfinance.gov to learn more. Keep in mind that debt laws and regulations vary by state. The material I discuss here is an overview of the main types of debt.

Total account	% of total assets
$5,000	3%
$27,000	17%
$31,000	20%
$9,000	6%
$8,000	5%
$12,500	8%
$14,000	9%
$24,000	16%
$24,500	16%
$155,000	100%
100%	

Secured Loans

Some debts, or loans, are secured, or backed by collateral. The most common form of a secured loan is a mortgage. With a mortgage, your home is the security, or collateral. If you purchase a home, put 20 percent down, and finance your home with a mortgage for the remaining 80 percent, the 20 percent that you put down is your **home equity**. Over time, the value of a home varies. The value of your home is based on what someone would be willing to pay for it today, rather than on the purchase price you paid plus improvements. If your home declines in value to below what you owe, your mortgage is considered **underwater**. A borrower whose mortgage is underwater has negative equity in his or her home.

If you **default** on your mortgage, or stop making payments, the lender can begin foreclosure proceedings and repossess your home. When a mortgage is underwater (the balance owed exceeds the value of the home), the lender may or may not be able to recoup the difference between the value of the home and the amount owed on the loan. Whether a loan is recourse or nonrecourse is a significant distinction. With a **recourse loan**, in the case of default, the lender can go after the borrower's other assets or garnish the borrower's wages. With a **nonrecourse loan**, the lender cannot go after the borrower's other assets in the case of default. In some states, mortgages are nonrecourse. In some of these states, mortgages are nonrecourse only if the loan was taken out when the home was purchased. Such loans are called **purchase money mortgages**. When you refinance your existing mortgage to get a better interest rate, the new loan is not a purchase money mortgage.

Another type of secured debt is a home equity loan or line of credit. With this kind of debt, the equity in the home is the security, or collateral. As the value of your home varies over time, so does your amount of home equity. To track the value of your home, look at comparable homes, or comps, in your neighborhood. Home equity loans usually require a current appraisal. A home equity loan may be a lump sum loan or it may be a line of credit. A **line of credit** means that the amount borrowed varies depending on how much you use it, or draw it down. A home equity line of credit is also called a **HELOC**.

There are differences between mortgages and home equity loans. A loan you take out to buy a home and a loan that you take out to refinance your purchase money mortgage, or your original mortgage, are both considered **first mortgages**. A home equity loan is considered a **second mortgage**. With a second mortgage, the first mortgage lender has priority over the second mortgage lender in the case of default. If a borrower defaults and the home is repossessed, the first mortgage lender gets paid first. Home equity loans are usually recourse loans, meaning the lender can go after the borrower's other assets.

Car loans and leases are secured loans. People may think of a car lease as an expense rather than as a debt obligation. But you should regard car leases as debts because they represent an obligation, just like a car loan or a mortgage. The monthly cost should appear as an expense on your income statement, and the total lease obligation should be included on your personal balance sheet as a liability, or debt.

Unsecured Loans

The most common type of unsecured loan is credit card debt. Credit cards are a line of credit, like a HELOC, because the amount outstanding varies. Even though there is no underlying security, or collateral, with a credit card, you should manage this type of credit card debt carefully. When it comes to credit cards, less is always more—and this applies to the number of cards as well as to the amount on them. Having too many credit card accounts hurts your credit score and makes it difficult to track the amount of your total debt.

Credit bureaus analyze your creditworthiness and assign you a credit score. Be mindful of things that could hurt your credit score, such as too much debt, opening and closing credit card accounts frequently, and late payments, or **delinquencies**. A low credit score means that you are considered a higher risk by the credit bureaus and will be charged a higher interest rate when you borrow money relative to those borrowers with a better credit profile.

In my opinion, store cards are unnecessary. You can use a store card in only one place. You might get some sort of benefit or discount when you open a store card account, but the act of opening the account has a negative impact on your credit score. Some store cards are actually charge cards and not credit cards. With a charge card, you must pay the balance in full each month.

In my midtwenties, I opened a charge card account at a department store that was near my office. Sometimes I ran to the store during lunch to pick up a few things, and checking out was faster with the card. Because it was a charge card, I received a bill only when I had a balance. When I moved to a new apartment, some of my mail was forwarded to the wrong address. I was busy with work and settling into my new apartment, and I didn't notice that I never received a bill for some purchases I had made on the charge card. I will never forget having my card declined the next time I tried to use it. Lesson learned. . . .

Instead of store cards, use one or two general credit cards that provide perks that are beneficial to you. Use a card that provides frequent flyer miles, cash back, or travel reward points. Consider using one credit card for automatic bills and keeping it in a safe place in your home. Carry a second credit card with you, and use it for all other purchases.

Student loans are also a type of unsecured debt. Public student loans are provided by the federal government, whereas private student loans are offered by banks, credit unions, and schools. Public loans often offer lower interest rates and have more flexible terms than private loans. Student loans are usually not **discharged**, or forgiven, in a bankruptcy.

Step 3: Evaluate Your Cash Flow

Your income statement and your balance sheet both provide useful information to help you analyze your financial profile. Evaluating your cash flow takes this information a step further. Unlike the income statement and balance sheet, cash flow takes into account changes in your savings and your debt.

You either consume or you save the money that you earn. The difference between income and consumption is your **net savings**.

If you	If you
Increase savings or	Reduce savings or
Reduce debt	Increase debt
~ Net savings will increase	~ Net savings will decrease

Regularly evaluating your cash flow relative to your income motivates you to factor in saving money and paying down debt. Mortgages, student loans, and car loans help you finance large expenditures by allowing you to pay for them over time, but how you handle these and other debts has a significant impact on your net worth. Along with saving for retirement and investing wisely, prudent management of your debts should be a priority. Thinking about the impact that financial choices have on your net worth helps you make better decisions.

Remember the formula assets minus liabilities equals net worth? Tables 3.4 and 3.5 show the impact that debt and savings decisions have on your net worth. In table 3.4, you use a credit card to finance a few large purchases that are not assets, such as a vacation, car repairs, braces, and sleep-away camp for the children. You then use your net income to pay off a large part of the credit card balance. Because the amount of the credit debt exceeds the net income earned that year, your net worth declines.

TABLE 3.4. Items affecting cash flow and net worth.		
Decrease in net savings and net worth		
Income	$88,000	
Net income	$9,500	
Use credit card for a few large purchases	–$12,000	
Pay down credit card with net income	$9,500	
	–$2,500	Decrease in net savings and net worth
Income	$88,000	
Consumption	$90,500	
Change in net savings	–$2,500	Consuming more than you earn

If you rely less on your credit card during the year, you could use the net income to pay off the entire credit card balance. You would also have money left over to supplement your savings. In this scenario, your net worth rises (table 3.5).

TABLE 3.5. Items affecting cash flow and net worth.

Increase in net savings and net worth

Income	$88,000	
Net income	$9,500	
Use credit card for a few large purchases	-$7,000	
Pay down debt and increase savings	$9,500	
	$2,500	Increase in net savings and net worth
Income	$88,000	
Consumption	$85,500	
Change in net savings	$2,500	Consuming less than you earn

Investors usually determine regular, or normalized, cash flow when they are analyzing a company. Normalized cash flow adjusts for, or backs out, any unusual inflows or outflows, such as a large unanticipated expense or a one-time gain. Adjusting for these unanticipated or one-time items, investors can get a clear view of a company's recurring, or regular, cash flow from day-to-day operations. You should look at your personal cash flow on a normalized basis. As you analyze your cash flow, adjust for unusual, or one-time, inflows or outflows, such as major car repairs following an auto accident or a special bonus at work.

It is particularly important to analyze your cash flow—not just your income—before making a big change, such as moving, buying a vacation home, having children, going from two incomes to one, or starting a business. Analyze both your current cash flow and your normalized cash flow as you face such transitions.

After you analyze your cash flow, you can identify ways to save money and grow your assets. Automatic savings plans, which you can use to save for retirement or for your children's education, are a relatively painless way to save. With automatic savings plans, the money goes directly into savings rather than into your checking account.

An advantage of automatic savings plans is that you can consistently invest the same dollar amount. When markets are strong and have appreciated, you invest in fewer shares of stock or of a mutual fund. When markets are weak, or values have fallen, the same dollar amount will allow you to buy more shares of stock or of a mutual fund. As a result, the average cost of your investment will be lower than if you decide to buy a set number of shares periodically. Investing a fixed-dollar amount at set intervals is called **dollar cost averaging**.

CHAPTER 4

Underwrite Yourself

THE NEXT TASK IN analyzing your financial profile is to underwrite yourself, or to assess the risk of your financial profile. **Underwriting** is what banks or insurance companies do when they evaluate risks associated with lending money or providing an insurance policy. To underwrite yourself, you need to take a close and honest look at your finances, ask yourself some questions, consider uncertainties and exposures, and evaluate your risk profile on many fronts. The steps in this chapter will help you analyze your financial profile in the same way that an objective third party would, highlighting areas that you might be able to change in order to reduce the financial risks in your life.

Step 1: Analyze Your Sources of Income

The first consideration is your income. Ask yourself these questions:

- Is your salary steady or variable?
- Do you rely on commissions or bonuses?
- Do you work in a cyclical industry?

If your compensation is variable, you should not carry a lot of debt. Likewise, you should make sure to have an ample cash reserve.

Step 2: Evaluate Your Debt

For companies and individuals, too much **leverage**, or debt, increases the riskiness of their financial profile. This section discusses some general principles to help you manage debt prudently.

Consumer Debt

When you are thinking of buying a big item, consider if you can actually afford the item, not just whether you can afford the payment. When you choose to finance a big item, you are adding a fixed obligation to your monthly expenses. What happens if your income goes down? You will have even less cushion and less flexibility than you currently do. Remember, if you borrow on your credit card to buy an item that is not an asset and is consumed—like a vacation—your net worth goes down. I love to travel and treasure my family vacations, but I do not use debt to pay for them. It is okay to use your credit card to pay for vacation expenses while you are away, as long as you make sure that you will be able to pay the balance in full upon your return.

Commit to paying off your credit card balances every month. Credit card interest rates can be very high, making it difficult to pay down a balance that has accumulated over time. Remember that your credit card debt is a liability on your personal balance sheet and affects your net worth.

Mortgages

Here are some general guidelines about mortgages:

* Do not buy a home that costs more than 2.5 times your annual income.

- Expenses such as interest, principal, taxes, real estate taxes, and insurance should not exceed 28 percent of your gross, or pretax, monthly income. This is called the **front-end ratio**.
- The combination of front-end ratio expenses plus all other fixed obligations, such as car payments, credit card bills, student loans, alimony, and child support, should not exceed 36 percent of gross, or pretax, monthly pay. This is called the **back-end ratio**.
- Don't buy a home unless you expect to live there for several years. A lot of expenses are associated with moving. Not only are closing costs and movers expensive, but outlays for improvements, furniture, and decorating can really add up.

Mortgage bankers and brokers are paid to help you finance your home. They may use different debt-to-income guidelines than are appropriate for your comfort level. Just because you have been approved for a mortgage for a particular amount doesn't mean that you need or should have a mortgage of that size.

Home Equity Loans

As with any debt, home equity loans can get you into trouble if they are not managed carefully. It is prudent to be approved for a home equity line of credit before you actually need to use it. Get approved when you don't need the money, because your financial profile will likely be better than when you actually do need the money. If you are approved for a home equity loan when your personal finances are in very good shape, you will be considered a low credit risk. If your circumstances change and you wait until you need the money to be approved, your financial profile may not be as solid. At that point, your credit profile will likely be riskier, you may be charged a higher interest rate, or you may not be approved.

Step 3: Have a Plan to Pay Off Debt

Always have a plan to reduce debt and always think in terms of net worth. All debt, even your mortgage, should be viewed as temporary. Aim to pay off your mortgage by the time you plan to retire. If you are not certain that you will be able to do that, your mortgage is probably too large. If you have an occasional inflow, such as a bonus or larger-than-expected tax refund, consider using some or all of it to pay down debt, especially credit card debt. Having a payoff plan, even for small debts, means that these obligations are less likely to become big worries.

After graduating from college, I was working a few days a week until I started my full-time job in January, so I borrowed money from my parents to help me get through those first few months. I lived very modestly and kept a tally of what I owed them on a bulletin board. Seeing the size of the debt every day kept me on track. Once I started paying my parents back, seeing my progress toward paying the debt down was great motivation to continue to do so.

Step 4: Examine Your Insurance Coverage

Insurance is a vital risk management tool and is a "must" in many areas of your life. You are required to have homeowners insurance if you have a mortgage and to have auto insurance in most states if you drive. If you rent your home, you should have renters insurance, even though it is not always required by landlords. Whether you own or rent your home, take pictures or videos of your possessions and store the images in a safe place. An ideal spot is with your vital papers in a safety deposit or fire-safe box. Consider whether you need an umbrella, or extra liability, policy, which goes beyond normal coverage. Depending on your circumstances, it might be appropriate.

Don't forget to consider life and disability insurance when you analyze your risk profile. In my opinion, term life insurance is usually more appropriate than whole life insurance. Whole life insurance provides coverage for your lifetime. With a whole life policy, there is certainty that you will die and that your beneficiaries will collect, and that certainty is reflected in the cost of the policy. Term life policies provide coverage for only a term, or for a certain period. Term life insurance is less expensive than whole life insurance because there is no certainty that you will die during the term of your policy. A term life policy can help protect your family if there is a loss of income due to the death of a parent. You can choose a policy term and amount that covers your family when your children are young and provides enough financial security to get your children through college and into their working years.

There are some situations, however, where whole life policies may be appropriate. If you have substantial assets and your heirs will likely owe estate taxes, whole life insurance might be a good idea—the insurance might be enough to cover estate taxes or other expenses. For example, if you own a business and die, your heirs will be left with an asset that may be quite valuable but is illiquid. Another situation in which to consider whole life insurance is if you have a dependent with special needs who will require financial support beyond your lifetime. For these situations, you should consult a financial planner—some financial planners focus on families with special-needs dependents.

Probability is a central component of assessing risk. For young people, the probability of becoming disabled is much higher than the probability of death. Therefore disability insurance is a good idea, especially for young families.

Life insurance agents often market life insurance as an investment. I am not a fan of insurance as an investment. Insurance carries fees, restrictions, and commissions. My advice is to use insurance to protect yourself from big risks and to use invest-ments to grow your money. Both insurance and investments have a place in your financial toolkit.

Step 5: Consider Other Risks and Exposures

Advances in technology and mobile communication have changed the way we manage our finances. These innovations save time and allow us to be more informed consumers. But the innova-tions have also introduced new risks and exposures.

Identity Theft and Fraud

Even if you are not shopping for a mortgage or car loan, review your credit report regularly. You are entitled to a free credit report once a year. You can download your free report and search for errors or indications of fraud at www.annualcre-ditreport.com.

If you will not be in the market for a new loan soon, it is pos-sible to freeze or lock your credit profile to reduce the chance of identity theft. In that case, you need to contact each of the three credit bureaus: Equifax, Experian, and TransUnion. Depending on what state you live in, there may be a fee to freeze your profile and another fee to unfreeze your profile. The fee is often waived if you have been the victim of identity theft.

Check the credit reports for your children to make sure that no one is using their identity. To access a credit report for your child, you need to request the report in writing from each bureau and provide proof of your child's identity and that you are the parent.

If you receive a suspicious email, text, or voicemail that appears to come from your credit card company, do not respond. These communications can appear official but are often from hackers. If you are ever unsure about communications from your credit card company, call the number on the back of your card.

Technological Risks

Given the amount of sensitive information traveling through your computer and mobile devices every day, you need to protect your data and limit access to it. Install updates regularly because they can provide the most current defense against viruses and malware.

There are a number of ways to enhance the security of your passwords. As tempting as it is, do not use the same password for everything. Create a variety of passwords with a mix of upper- and lowercase letters, symbols, and numbers. Use a pass phrase rather than a password. A pass phrase is longer and includes more characters than a password. The more characters in your password or pass phrase, the harder it is for someone to figure it out.

Consider using a password site to keep your passwords organized and secure. I have found that it is far easier to remember one master password or pass phrase than a unique password for every site. Password management services often flag passwords that are too simple and therefore not secure. Some will even generate passwords for you.

A handwritten list of passwords can be secure, as long as you keep the list in a safe place away from your computer. Whatever method you decide to use, never instruct your browser or a website to remember a password. If your laptop is stolen, it will be much easier for someone to gain access to your accounts if your passwords are saved in the browser.

In addition to a password management site, I use an online service to back up my computer files regularly. It is also a good idea to back up computer files using an external hard drive. Backed-up files can be saved in a fire-safe box or a safety deposit box at your bank. Never leave sensitive information on a hard drive.

. . . .

A friend had saved a copy of her tax return on her laptop's hard drive. The laptop was stolen. Think of all the information contained on your tax return. Pretty scary. . . .

. . . .

A Note on Risk Tolerance

When you underwrite yourself, you need to be objective and consider how another person would assess the riskiness of your financial profile. Be honest with yourself so you can identify areas where you might be able to make changes and alter the risk associated with your finances. This is known as **risk management**.

In contrast to risk management, **risk tolerance** is about personal preferences. It is about how comfortable you are taking on risk. The riskiness of different investment choices varies. The next section covers fundamental investing concepts, types of investments, and types of investment accounts. Just as you need to be honest and objective about the riskiness of your financial profile, you need to be honest and objective about your comfort level with different degrees of volatility, or risk. As you consider if you want to be conservative, moderate, or aggressive with your investments, think about your time horizon. Think about liquidity. Last, and perhaps most important, talk with your partner. No two people are exactly alike. When it comes to your family's finances, you and your partner should be on the same page.

PART 3

Educate Yourself About Investing

An investment in knowledge pays the best interest.

—BENJAMIN FRANKLIN

. . . .

This section delves into investing concepts, asset classes, how to invest, and types of investment accounts. It covers a broad range of topics; as you read through these chapters, keep in mind that not all investable assets or accounts will be appropriate for you. Each investor's needs and goals are unique.

. . . .

CHAPTER 5

Some Fundamental Concepts

O UNDERSTAND INVESTING, you must know about some fundamental concepts. These concepts will help you become a more informed and successful investor. Some have been introduced already; others will be new. These fundamental concepts

Investable Assets *What to Invest In*	Investment Structures *Ways to Invest*	Investment Accounts *Why to Invest*
• Cash and money market • Bonds • Equities • Derivatives • Master limited partnerships (MLPs) • Real estate investment trusts (REITs) • Private capital • Alternative assets • Commodities and currencies	• Individual account • Mutual funds • Index funds • Exchange traded funds (ETFs) • Exchange traded notes (ETNs) • Target date funds	• Taxable • 401(k) and 403(b) • IRA • Roth IRA and 401(k) • Annuities • 529 plans

Fundamental Investing Concepts

Figure 5.1. Fundamental investing concepts.

will provide a foundation for understanding investments, markets, and investment strategies.

Supply and Demand

Supply and demand play a central role in investing. The value of an item depends not on what you paid for it, but on what someone else would be willing to pay for it today. Four principles are tied to supply and demand, as demonstrated in table 5.1.

TABLE 5.1. Supply and demand.

Supply and demand: Four principles

If ...	And ...	Then	Example
There is a fixed supply of something			
	Demand increases	Price will rise	After an artist dies, the prices of existing works go up.
	Demand decreases	Price will decline	A retailer cuts the price of an out-of-style item to move inventory.
There is a fixed demand for something			
	Supply increases	Price will decline	When a fad is overproduced and is widely available, retailers will have to cut prices.
	Supply decreases	Price will rise	The prices of agricultural products rise following a drought.

Yield, Total Return, and Compounding

For any asset, **yield** is the income earned divided by the price of the asset, such as a bond or a share of stock. Price and yield move in opposite directions, a concept that can be a little confusing. If the

price of an asset goes down, then the yield goes up. If the price of
an asset rises, then the yield declines. Let's walk through the math.

- If a $1,000 bond earns 5 percent interest, it earns $50 on a
  $1,000 asset, or $50 divided by $1,000, which is a 5 percent
  yield. If the price of the bond increases to $1,050, the
  yield declines to $50 on a $1,050 asset, or 4.8 percent. The
  income for a bond is fixed, so changes in yield are always
  driven by changes in the demand for—and market price
  of—a particular bond.

$$\$50 \div \$1,000 = 5.0\% \quad \text{and} \quad 50 \div \$1,050 = 4.8\%$$

- If a share of stock is worth $50 and pays a $1 dividend per
  share, the yield is $1 divided by $50, or 2 percent. Stock
  yields fluctuate depending on the demand for—and market
  price of—a particular stock. If the stock declines in value
  to $45, then the yield increases to 2.2 percent. If a company
  increases its dividend, then the yield will also change. Raising the dividend to $1.10 results in a 2.2 percent yield.

$$\$1 \div \$50 = 2.0\% \quad \text{and} \quad 1 \div \$45 = 2.2\% \quad \text{and} \quad 1.10 \div \$50 = 2.2\%$$

Total return is the combination of yield and the change in
valuation. Total return takes into account the income earned
on an investment, such as interest or dividends, and any appreciation or depreciation in the value of the asset. If a stock earns
a 2 percent dividend yield and appreciates 5 percent in a year,
the total return is 7 percent.

2% dividend yield + 5% appreciation = 7% total return

Compounding means that there is growth on the growth.
The compounding of returns has a significant impact on the
value of investments over time. For example, an investment of
$100 with appreciation of 7 percent will be worth $107 at the end
of the first year. If the investment appreciates 7 percent again in

the second year, the return would be 7 percent on $107, or $7.49. At the end of the second year, the investment would be worth $107 plus $7.49, or $114.49. In the second year, the increase in the value of the investment of $7.49 is greater than the increase in year 1 of $7.00 because of the growth on the growth.

7% growth on $100 = $107 and 7% growth on $107 = $114.49

Risk

In the investing world, **risk** is the variability, or volatility, of investment returns. **Volatility** is measured by the dispersion, or the standard deviation, of outcomes, or returns. The **standard deviation** is how far an actual return might be from the average, or expected, return for a particular investment. With investments, the greater the standard deviation, the greater the risk.

The weather is a good illustration of standard deviation. A forecast gives an average, or expected, temperature for a city on a particular day of the year. In some regions, such as Southern

Sell in May and Go Away

Historically, the level of trading activity, or volume, in the stock market declines during the summer months compared with the rest of the year. Reduced trading volume can sometimes lead to greater volatility in stock prices. In some years, the market has not performed well during the summer months. The adage "Sell in May and go away" suggests that investors should sell investments in May and sit on cash throughout the summer. This is not a recommended strategy, however. You should not try to move in and out of the market, or time the market. Rather, you should have a long-term orientation. That said, be careful not to buy or sell during any period with significantly low trading activity. There can be greater volatility on a slow trading day, such as the day before a holiday or the Friday after Thanksgiving.

California, there is less variability, or volatility, in temperature for a particular day of the year. In other areas, such as Chicago, there is much more variability, or volatility, in temperature for a particular day of the year. Thus, the standard deviation in weather for a particular day of the year is greater in Chicago than it is in Southern California.

Investors are compensated for taking risk. In other words, as risk or volatility rises, so should the anticipated return. Volatility, or the standard deviation of returns, varies depending on the type of investment. It also depends on the amount of trading activity for that asset. If there is less trading activity, or trading volume, volatility will increase.

- -

If you are investing in mutual funds, it is helpful to look at the standard deviation for each of your choices. Comparing standard deviations gives you a sense of the relative riskiness of each option. This information is available on Morningstar.com. If you want to do in-depth research on funds or any other investments and have a library card, you can usually access Morningstar and other investment resources for free at your local public library.

- -

Bullish or Bearish

The terms *bullish* and *bearish* are used to describe an outlook for financial markets. A bull thrusts his horns up when he does battle. A bear swings his or her arms down in a fight. If you are bullish, you think that the market will rise. The term *bull market* is often used to describe a continuous period of rising values. If you are bearish, you think that the market will go down. A *correction* is often used to describe a decline of 10 percent or more in the market. Some investors refer to a decline of more than 20 percent as a *bear market*. Investors often track the amount of time since the last correction and since the last bear market.

Liquidity

Liquidity reflects how easily an asset can be converted to cash. In general, investable assets, such as stocks and bonds, are more liquid than other assets. College savings plans and retirement savings accounts are less liquid than other types of investment accounts because there are penalties for withdrawing money early. Real estate assets are normally classified as illiquid—you cannot necessarily sell your home at any given time.

Assets that are less liquid can decline in value significantly during a financial crisis. During periods of economic turmoil, illiquid assets, such as homes or condos, can become even more illiquid. When many people are selling assets, whether it is a stock or a home, illiquidity makes the situation more challenging. In a financial crisis, investors may have to sell what they can rather than selling lower-quality assets that they should.

Do not plan to use investable assets that are illiquid or could fluctuate in value to pay for large obligations like tuition or taxes that are due soon. Rather, fund these near-term obligations with the most liquid, least volatile assets that you have access to, such as cash or money market funds.

Concentration and Diversification

The saying "Don't put all your eggs in one basket" applies to investments, because concentration increases risk. Whether you invest your money yourself or work with a professional, never put all your assets in the same basket—the same kind of stock, bond, mutual fund, or other investment.

In addition to avoiding concentration, diversification is key to improving investment results. Various asset classes, or types of investments, tend to perform differently under certain market conditions—some perform better, and some perform worse, depending on what is going on with the economy and financial markets. The best investment strategy is to have a diverse portfolio that includes a mixture of US stocks, international stocks, US bonds, and international bonds.

Diversification across asset classes helps reduce risk; correlation illustrates this benefit. **Correlation** measures how things, such as investment returns, move in relation to each other. Some asset class returns are more correlated than others. Say you invest in a stock and in a bond. If the economy picks up steam, corporate earnings will likely rise and so will your stock. As the economy picks up steam, however, the Federal Reserve may raise interest rates to keep inflation in check. When the Federal Reserve raises rates, the value of the bond that you hold will decline. Another investor could get a higher interest rate on a new bond issued today because rates are now higher in the market. The decline in the value of your bond is offset to some degree by the increase in the value of your stock. Hence the benefit of diversification.

Not only should you diversify across asset classes, you should diversify within asset classes. Invest in different types of stocks and different types of bonds. An easy way to diversify is to invest in companies that are different sizes. **Capitalization**, or cap, is the market value of all shares of stock outstanding. There are small-cap, midcap, and large-cap stocks. Here are some general definitions:

- Small-cap companies have market valuations of less than $2 billion to $3 billion, and microcap companies have even smaller market valuations of less than $500 million.
- Large-cap companies are usually market valuations of greater than $10 billion to $15 billion. Megacap companies are even larger and have market valuations of greater than $50 billion to $100 billion.
- Midcap companies fall between large and small caps.

Changes in the economy and changes in the financial markets can have different impacts on large-cap stocks than on small-cap stocks. Therefore, diversifying across market capitalization ranges lowers the risk of your investment profile (figure 5.2).

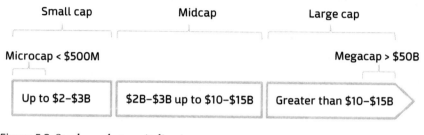

Figure 5.2. Stock market capitalization ranges.

Fees

The impact of fees over the life of an investment or the life of an investment account can be significant, so an understanding of fees is essential. In the investment arena, fees are usually charged as a percentage of assets. They are often quoted in terms of basis points. A **basis point** is one one-hundredth of 1 percent, or 0.01 percent. In other words, 100 basis points equals 1.0 percent, and 50 basis points equals one-half of 1 percent, or 0.50 percent.

There are many kinds of fees. Some fees are transaction based: these are paid to brokers as compensation for putting clients in an investment or for executing a trade. Examples of transaction-based fees are commissions and sales loads. With a commission, the brokerage firm charges a fee for each transaction. A **sales load** is a one-time front-end or back-end fee that goes to the brokerage firm that is selling you a mutual fund. A front-end load is a reduction to the initial investment. If you

make a $100 investment with a 5 percent sales load, you are put-
ting only $95 to work. A back-end load is a reduction of pro-
ceeds. If you sell a $100 investment with a 5 percent back-end
load, you receive $95. Not all mutual funds have sales loads.
Discount and online brokerage firms offer a large number of
no-load funds.

In contrast to brokers, who charge commissions and loads,
fee-based advisers are paid an annual fee based on a percentage
of assets under management. The adviser is not paid to exe-
cute trades. Rather, he or she is paid to invest your money. If the
investments perform well, the portfolio grows, and the financial
adviser also does well. Unlike brokers, who charge transaction-
based fees, incentives are aligned for fee-based financial advisers and their clients. Advisory fees traditionally average around
1 percent, and often range from 0.75 percent up to 1.75 percent.
For larger accounts, fees may be lower. Competition from online
financial planning models has helped bring down fees.

For mutual funds, the management fee depends on the type
of fund. According to the Investment Company Institute, Lip-
per, and Morningstar, the average annual stock fund management fee in 2016 was 63 basis points. For bond funds, the average annual management fee was 51 basis points. Management
fees have been coming down. Twenty years ago, the average
fee was 104 basis points for stock funds and 84 basis points for
bonds funds.[6]

Compared with the averages just mentioned, fees are higher
for smaller cap funds and international funds. Researching
small-cap and international stocks tends to be more expensive
than researching large-cap US-based stocks. Traveling, visiting
management teams, and learning about products and customers can be challenging if the company is not easily accessible or
if little is known about the company. Some small-company or
international stocks are **below the radar**, or not well-known by

most investors. This can be a good thing if the fund finds hidden gems that are undervalued.

Fees are lower for index funds and for exchange-traded funds, or ETFs. Depending on the type of index fund or ETF, the fee may be less than 10 basis points. More specialized index funds have a slightly higher fee. These types of investments are covered in greater detail in the next chapter.

Table 5.2 illustrates the long-term impact of fees. For example, $1,000 earning a 7 percent return will grow to $4,322 after thirty years if the investment is in a fund charging 2 percent. That same $1,000 earning 7 percent would grow to $6,614 after thirty years if the fund charged only 0.50 percent.

Although investment fees may seem complicated, they are important to understand because of their impact on the growth of your money. If you meet with a prospective financial advisor, fees should be an important part of the discussion. In a mutual fund prospectus, fees are noted in the table of contents. Fees are also listed on Morningstar, online brokerage firms' websites, and the various mutual fund marketplaces. Make sure you understand all fees, whether you invest on your own or through a broker or adviser.

Tax Efficiency

As an investor, you need to consider the impact of taxes. The taxes owed on an investment depend on the type of investment account that is holding the investment. For **tax-deferred accounts**, such as 401(k)s and 403(b)s, you do not pay taxes on the income or capital gains generated each year. Instead, you pay taxes when you withdraw money from the account. Roth IRAs and college savings plans, such as 529s, are examples of a **tax-advantaged account**. You fund it with after-tax dollars, but the income, appreciation, and withdrawals are tax free. For **taxable**

TABLE 5.2. Long-term impact of fees on an investment.			
Annual investment return	7.0%		
Initial investment	$1,000		
	Year-end balance at different fee rates		
Year	2.0%	1.0%	0.5%
1	$1,050	$1,060	$1,065
2	$1,103	$1,124	$1,134
3	$1,158	$1,191	$1,208
4	$1,216	$1,262	$1,286
5	$1,276	$1,338	$1,370
6	$1,340	$1,419	$1,459
7	$1,407	$1,504	$1,554
8	$1,477	$1,594	$1,655
9	$1,551	$1,689	$1,763
10	$1,629	$1,791	$1,877
11	$1,710	$1,898	$1,999
12	$1,796	$2,012	$2,129
13	$1,886	$2,133	$2,267
14	$1,980	$2,261	$2,415
15	$2,079	$2,397	$2,572
16	$2,183	$2,540	$2,739
17	$2,292	$2,693	$2,917
18	$2,407	$2,854	$3,107
19	$2,527	$3,026	$3,309
20	$2,653	$3,207	$3,524
21	$2,786	$3,400	$3,753
22	$2,925	$3,604	$3,997
23	$3,072	$3,820	$4,256
24	$3,225	$4,049	$4,533
25	$3,386	$4,292	$4,828
26	$3,556	$4,549	$5,141
27	$3,733	$4,822	$5,476
28	$3,920	$5,112	$5,832
29	$4,116	$5,418	$6,211
30	$4,322	$5,743	$6,614
Difference		$1,421	$2,292

Note: Assumes that the initial investment was made at the beginning
of the year.

accounts, income and capital gains are not tax exempt or tax deferred, so you owe taxes each year. Tax efficiency means that you are managing a taxable account in a way that minimizes the taxes owed each year. For any investment, the tax treatment for the income and gains depends on a number of factors.

Capital Gains and Losses

A **capital gain** or **capital loss** is the difference between the cost basis of an investment and what is received when the investment is sold. Remember that the cost basis is the original amount paid for an investment plus or minus any adjustments to the original cost that occur while you hold the investment.

For assets that have appreciated, you pay taxes on capital gains when you sell the asset. There are some important considerations to keep in mind with respect to taxes on investment gains and losses. Short-term capital gains occur when an appreciated investment is held for one year or less. Long-term gains occur when an appreciated investment is held for at least one year plus one day. Tax rates for short-term gains are much higher than they are for long-term gains. Short-term gains are taxed as ordinary income at a rate that can be as high as 37 percent, depending on your tax bracket. **Ordinary income** is the tax rate that you pay on your wages or salary and on interest and other sources of income. Depending on where you live, state taxes may also apply.

Investors who have taxable income above a certain amount also pay a **net investment income tax**, or **NIIT**, of 3.8 percent, for a total rate as high as 40.8 percent. The rate for long-term gains can be as high as 23.8 percent, or 20 percent plus 3.8 percent with the NIIT.

When investors take, or **realize**, a loss on an investment, they can use that loss to offset some or all of the capital gains they have realized on other investments. As an investor, you should keep track of gains and losses as you incur them and try to offset your gains with losses, especially as year-end draws near. It is also possible to carry losses forward to offset gains in the future. The amount of losses that you can carry over each year, however, is limited. You cannot realize a capital loss in the event of a **wash sale**, which occurs when an investor sells an investment to realize a loss and buys it back within thirty days.

Taxes on Dividends

For taxable accounts, the treatment of dividends depends on whether they are **qualified** or **nonqualified**. Most US company dividends are qualified and are taxed at the same rate as long-term capital gains. Depending on your income, these rates can be as high as 20.0 percent. Dividends from foreign companies and REITs (real estate investment trusts) are nonqualified. Investment income from nonqualified sources is taxed at the ordinary income rate, which can be as high as 37 percent.

If you do not rely on income from your investments to help you live day-to-day, you should focus on investments that appreciate in value, rather than those that generate interest and dividends. For investments that generate interest and dividends, also called **current income**, you will pay taxes each year. With appreciated securities, you decide when you want to sell and pay capital gains.

Benefit of Donating Appreciated Securities

If you own stocks that have increased in value significantly, consider using them for donations. Donating appreciated securities allows you to avoid paying capital gains taxes. The value of the donation is based on the market value on the date of the gift. If you sell the asset and donate the cash, you will have to pay capital gains. You need to have owned the investment for more than one year to get the full benefit. In addition, you will need to provide the cost basis for tax returns, so keep good records. If you decide to donate securities, choose holdings that have the lowest cost basis relative to the current market value. These securities will provide the biggest tax benefit.

My friend has a small family business. All family members involved in the business have whole life insurance policies. When the life insurance company demutualized many years ago, each family member received shares of the insurance company's stock. Over the years, the stock appreciated. These shares were perfect for donation because they had a very low cost basis.

CHAPTER 6

Investable Assets: What to Invest In

N OW THAT YOU ARE familiar with some fundamental concepts involved in investing, let's delve into the various asset classes—how they work, what affects their value, and the types of investments that are available.

Investable Assets *What to Invest In*	Investment Structures *Ways to Invest*	Investment Accounts *Why to Invest*
• Cash and money market • Bonds • Equities • Derivatives • Master limited partnerships (MLPs) • Real estate investment trusts (REITs) • Private capital • Alternative assets • Commodities and currencies	• Individual account • Mutual funds • Index funds • Exchange traded funds (ETFs) • Exchange traded notes (ETNs) • Target date funds	• Taxable • 401(k) and 403(b) • IRA • Roth IRA and 401(k) • Annuities • 529 plans

Fundamental Investing Concepts

Figure 6.1. Investable assets.

The Capital Markets

Before we discuss asset classes, let's begin with the **capital markets**, commonly referred to as the financial markets. Investors provide money, or **capital**, to companies, governments, and municipalities. In exchange for providing money, or capital, investors expect to earn a return. Companies, governments, and municipalities use capital for a variety of reasons. For example, a company may use short-term capital to finance short-term needs, such as inventory or accounts receivable. A municipality may use long-term capital to fund longer-term needs, such as buildings, equipment, and infrastructure such as roads or bridges.

Let's look at how a company raises capital. Companies can raise money by **issuing debt**, or selling bonds to investors, or by **issuing equity**, or selling stock. A key distinction between the two methods of raising capital is that a bond is an obligation, or debt; stock, or equity, represents ownership. Bondholders have priority over, or are senior to, equity shareholders. In other words, if a company is in financial distress, bondholders will be paid before shareholders.

The capital markets encompass both the primary market and the secondary market. When companies issue new stock or new bonds to raise capital, the stock or bonds are sold in the **primary market**. In an **initial public offering**, or **IPO**, investors buy stock or bonds from the company, or issuer. After an initial public offering, investors buy or sell stock and bonds from each other. This is called the **secondary market**. Trading—buying and selling securities—takes place on exchanges. The capital markets are interconnected around the globe.

When a company issues stock or bonds in the primary market, some investors may choose to hang on to their stock or bonds, and others may choose to sell their stock or bonds to other investors in the secondary market. As investors begin buying or selling stock and bonds in the secondary market, the value of what people hold changes. Remember the fundamental concept that the value of what you own does not depend on what you paid for it, but rather on what someone else is willing to pay for it today.

There are two main types of investors in the capital markets. **Retail investors** are individuals who act on their own behalf. When you invest your savings, either by yourself or with a broker or financial adviser, you are considered a retail investor. **Institutional investors** manage money for others. Examples of institutional investors are mutual funds, insurance companies, endowments, foundations, and pension plans.

Most Common Types of Investable Assets

Now that you have had a brief introduction to the capital markets, let's take a look at different types of investable assets, how they work, and what causes them to increase or decrease in value. We'll start with the most commonly held investable assets.

Cash and Money Market Funds

The most liquid asset is cash in a checking or savings account. You can access cash from an ATM twenty-four hours a day, seven days a week. Banks also offer **certificates of deposit,** or **CDs,** as an alternative to savings accounts. Like savings accounts, CDs are insured by the Federal Deposit Insurance Company, or FDIC. With a checking or savings account, you have total control over your money; with a CD, the bank has the use of your money for a specific amount of time, or **term.** You can withdraw your money before the end of the CD's term, but there is a penalty. Banks also offer **money market deposit accounts** that are

FDIC insured. These accounts are like savings accounts, but they allow you to write checks. There is usually a limit to the number of transactions allowed over a period of time.

FDIC Insurance: What Is Covered, What Is Not?

As of this writing, FDIC insurance coverage is limited to $250,000 per account. The limits depend on the type of account—whether it is a joint account or an individual account. The FDIC does not cover securities, such as stocks, bonds, money market funds, annuities, or mutual funds, even if they are offered by a bank. Visit www.fdic.gov to learn more.

Money market funds invest in high-quality, very short-term, liquid securities like short-term government debt, CDs, and short-term municipal bonds. Unlike money market deposit accounts, money market funds are not FDIC insured.

Bonds

When you invest in a bond, you are loaning money to an entity, or an **issuer**, for a specific amount of time. The various types of issuers include companies, municipalities, the US government, and foreign governments. Remember that bonds pay investors interest at a fixed amount, which is why bonds are also known as **fixed-income securities**.

The two components of bonds are principal and interest. **Principal** is the face value of the bond, and it is the amount returned to you when the bond matures. Interest on the principal is paid periodically, usually semiannually, over the life, or term, of the bond. At the end of the term, or when the bond matures, the issuer pays the final interest payment and returns the principal.

For example, if you invest in a $1,000 face value bond with a five-year term and 4 percent interest payable semiannually, you will receive an interest payment of $20 every six months for five years. At the end of the five-year term, you will also receive $1,000—the face value of the bond—along with the final interest payment of $20.

Coupons

Interest payments are sometimes called coupons. In the old days, investors pulled a coupon off a bond and submitted it to the issuer to collect an interest payment. Interest payments are now paid electronically, but you might still hear the word.

FACTORS THAT AFFECT A BOND'S VALUE

Bonds are valued based on the expected receipt of interest payments and principal over the term of the bond and the relative riskiness of that stream of payments. Changes at the company, in the financial markets, and in the US and foreign economies all can affect a bond's value. Over time, as bonds trade in the secondary market, the value increases or decreases depending on the credit worthiness, or credit quality, of the issuer and current economic and market conditions. If a bond trades at face value, it is at **par**. Bonds can also trade at a premium or a discount to par.

Credit risk. A change in the creditworthiness of the issuer (positive or negative) will affect a bond's value. If the issuer, such as a company or government entity, becomes less creditworthy, the bond declines in value. If a company's financial condition deteriorates to the point where the issuer stops paying interest (or principal), it is in default.

To issue debt, an issuer needs a credit rating. Rating agencies conduct an independent analysis of the issuer and assign a credit rating. To indicate a top rating, S&P and Fitch use AAA, or "triple A," and Moody's uses Aaa. The top rating is followed by AA, or "double A," A or "single A," BBB, BB, B, CCC, CC, C, and then D. There are also distinctions such as plus, or +, and minus, or –. For example, AAA is followed by AA+, and then AA, and then AA–, and so on.

The higher the credit rating, the lower the perceived credit risk. The lower the credit risk, the lower the interest rate that an issuer needs to pay investors. AAA ratings are rare. Very few companies and approximately a dozen countries have a AAA rating. In the US, only two companies—Johnson & Johnson and Microsoft— have AAA ratings. US government debt is currently rated AA+. Any bond rated BB or lower is considered noninvestment grade. These are also referred to as **speculative**, or **junk, bonds**.

Bond prices are quoted as a spread over Treasury bonds, or Treasuries. Treasuries are very low-risk investments and are backed by the full faith and credit of the United States. The difference between the yield on a bond and the interest rate for a Treasury bond with the same maturity is the **spread**.

bond yield – Treasury bond yield = spread

The riskier the credit, the wider the spread. For example, if a ten-year Treasury bond is trading at 3 percent and a ten-year corporate bond is trading at 6 percent, the spread is 3 percent, or 300 basis points. For a less risky issuer with a higher credit rating, the yield on a ten-year bond might be 5.5 percent, or a spread of 2.5 percent, or 250 basis points. Spreads across the board can vary depending on how optimistic investors are about the future. If investors have a positive economic outlook, spreads will tend to be narrower. If investors are more pessimistic, bond spreads will widen across the board.

Interest rate risk. Interest rates are determined by how much money is needed to compensate someone for borrowing his or her money. Interest rates also factor in expectations about inflation. If the expectation is for fast economic growth, interest rates will likely increase. If the growth rate of the US economy accelerates, the Federal Reserve is more likely to raise rates to keep inflation in check. Remember that with higher inflation, the dollars received back are worth less. Therefore, during an inflationary period, investors demand higher rates.

If Market Interest Rates	Or Credit Quality	A Bond's Value	A Bond's Yield
Decrease	Improves	Rises	Declines
Increase	Deteriorates	Declines	Rises

If interest rates rise after you invest in a bond, the bond's value will decline. Because an investor could get a higher interest rate in the market for a new bond, demand for your bond will go down, and your bond will trade at a discount. Likewise, if an issuer becomes less creditworthy after you invest, or if the rating agencies downgrade the issuer's credit rating, the bond will be worth less. The credit risk has increased, and other investors are not willing to pay as much as you did for the bond. If demand for the bond declines, due to higher interest rates available in the market or to declining credit quality, the value of the bond will decline, and the yield will increase. If the bond's value drops to $950, the yield will increase to $50 on $950, or 5.3 percent.

Duration measures how a bond's price is affected by a change in interest rates. Duration depends on the timing of the two types of payments received from a bond: interest payments and the principal payment at maturity. Duration is expressed in years.

All things equal, a longer term until maturity will mean a longer duration. If two bonds have the same face value, or principal amount, and the same term, the one with the higher interest rate will have the shorter duration. In this case, you would receive more of the cash stream sooner than you would with the bond that has the lower stated interest rate and smaller periodic interest payments.

You could also have two bonds with the same face value and interest rates but with different maturities. A longer maturity generally means a longer duration. More of the cash flow is received by the bondholder later in the term compared to a bond with a shorter maturity.

Understanding duration is important because duration determines volatility. The shorter the duration, the lower the interest rate volatility. The longer the duration, the greater the interest rate volatility. If you think interest rates will rise, invest in shorter duration bonds rather than in longer duration bonds. In a rising rate environment, a bond with a longer maturity will decline in value more than a shorter maturity bond will. Longer duration is not always a bad thing, however. If you expect interest rates to drop, invest in longer duration bonds. If you already own a bond that is paying a higher interest rate than is available for new bonds, you will receive a greater number of higher-than-market interest payments.

Duration helps to approximate the fluctuations in a bond's value in a rising or declining interest rate environment. As an illustration, if a bond has a duration of five years and rates increase by 1 percent, the value of the bond should decline by 5 x 1.0 percent, or 5 percent. For the same bond, a 1 percent decline in rates should increase the value of the bond by 5 x 1.0 percent, or 5 percent.

TYPES OF BONDS

There are different types of bonds, and the type of bond depends on the type of issuer. **Corporate bonds**, or **corporates**, are issued by companies. Bonds issued by companies based in the United States are called **domestic bonds**. In addition to credit risk and interest rate risk, the value of bonds issued by international companies is driven by changes in the value of the currency.

Here's an illustration of the impact of currency fluctuations on an international investment. If you are a US citizen and you invest in a corporate bond issued by a company based in Germany, the company, or issuer, will pay you interest in euros. If the euro strengthens, or appreciates, relative to the dollar, €1 costs more relative to $1. When you receive your interest payment in euros and convert them to dollars, you will receive more dollars than you would have if the euro had not appreciated. In contrast, if the euro weakens relative to the dollar, the interest payments in euros will be worth less in dollars.

Treasuries include all types and maturities of debt issued by the federal government. **Treasury bills** have maturities of less than one year, **Treasury notes** have maturities of between one and ten years, and **Treasury bonds** have maturities of ten years or longer. Interest on Treasury bills, notes, and bonds is exempt from state and local taxes. Interest on Treasury bills, notes, and bonds is not exempt from federal taxes.

Municipal bonds are issued by states or local governments, and there are two types. **General obligation bonds** represent general debts of a municipality. **Revenue bonds** are issued to fund a municipal project and use revenue tied to a specific source of income, such as a toll road, to make interest payments. Interest earned on most municipal bonds is exempt from federal taxation and from state and local taxation if the investor resides in the locale that issued the bond. If you invest in a municipal bond mutual fund, interest is not tax exempt. We will discuss mutual funds in the next chapter.

Sovereign bonds are issued by foreign governments. As with international corporate bonds, currency fluctuations can have an impact on sovereign bond returns.

Equity, or Stock

Equity represents ownership. When a company issues equity, or **stock**, to raise capital, investors buy a piece of that company and are entitled to a share of the company's earnings. Remember that bondholders are senior to equity shareholders, or have priority. If a company is in financial distress, interest and principal are paid to bondholders before anything is paid to shareholders. This is an important distinction in a bankruptcy.

WHAT AFFECTS VALUE

Investment returns and the volatility of returns have an impact on the value of a stock and are the result of both market-specific and company-specific factors. Market-specific factors, such as the domestic economic outlook, politics, changes in US tax policy, and international forces, all have an impact on the value of equities. Company-specific factors include product launches, competitive advantages, competitive threats, and changes in management. If a company's earnings rise or fall, the value of the stock rises or falls. If expectations about the company's future earnings become better or worse, the stock rises or falls.

How a stock—or portfolio of stocks—performs relative to the overall market is a measure of volatility. Analyzing beta is one way to look at the expected investment performance of a stock. **Beta** indicates how a stock tends to perform relative to the overall market and is determined using historical returns:

- A beta of 1.0 means that a stock's performance is expected to move exactly like the market or like a broad index, such as the S&P 500. If the S&P 500 is up 10 percent, the stock can be expected to rise 10 percent.
- A beta of 1.5 means that if the S&P 500 is up 10 percent, the stock should rise more than the market, or an increase of 15 percent. If the S&P 500 is down 10 percent, the stock can be expected to decline 15 percent. A higher beta means greater relative volatility.

This is a good thing in up markets and a bad thing in down markets.

- A beta of 0.5 means that the stock moves less than the market. If the S&P 500 is up 10 percent, the stock can be expected to rise only 5 percent. A lower beta means lower volatility, which is a good thing in down markets and a bad thing in up markets.
- A beta of 0 means that the performance of the investment is completely unrelated to, or uncorrelated with, the market.
- Beta can be negative, indicating that a stock's performance is expected to move in the opposite direction of the market. If the market rises, the stock will fall. Negative beta is uncommon.

You can also assess the volatility of a portfolio of stocks or a stock mutual fund by looking at the beta for the portfolio or fund. The beta for a portfolio or fund is based on a weighted average beta for all the stocks. With a weighted average, the beta for a holding representing 5 percent of the portfolio will be weighted by 5 percent to determine the weighted average beta for the portfolio. You can find the beta for a stock on most financial websites and beta for a fund on Morningstar.

The return on an investment is a combination of beta and alpha. **Alpha** illustrates how much of the return is not explained by beta. For example, if the beta for a stock is 1.0, the S&P 500 rises 10 percent, and the stock increases 12 percent, the alpha is 2 percent. In other words, the investment performed relatively better than expected given its beta. If the beta of a stock is 1.5, the S&P 500 rises 10 percent, and the investment increases 12 percent, the alpha is –3 percent. In this case, the investment return is positive, but it underperformed relative to expectations.

VALUATION METRICS

To determine whether a stock's valuation is attractive, investors consider a number of ratios, or valuation metrics. Investors can compare a stock's valuation metrics to that of other companies in the industry, to the company's peers, or to the overall market using a financial website such as Yahoo Finance or Morningstar or on a brokerage firm's website.

Price/earnings ratio. A common measure is the **price/earnings ratio**, or the price of a share of stock divided by the stock's **earnings per share**. Earnings per share equals a company's net income divided by the total shares outstanding. Shares outstanding are all stock that has been issued by the company that has been sold to investors or is held by insiders. If a company earns $10,000,000 and has 5,000,000 shares outstanding, then earnings per share would be $2.

The price/earnings ratio, also known as the **P/E multiple**, or **P/E**, reflects how much an investor is willing to pay for one share of a company's earnings. For example, if a share of stock is trading at $20 and earnings are $2 per share, the P/E is $20/$2, or 10x. In other words, the investor is willing to pay ten times earnings.

The price/earnings ratio is reported two ways. Earnings per share can be based on what the company earned in the past twelve months, known as the **trailing twelve months P/E**. Earnings per share may also be based on a consensus estimate of what Wall Street investment analysts expect the company to earn over the next year, known as the **forward P/E**.

Long-term earnings growth. Investors are willing to pay a higher valuation for stocks with stronger earnings growth potential. When investors evaluate a stock as a potential investment, they are looking at what they would pay for one share of what a company is expected to earn this year. In addition, investors are considering what the company is expected to earn next year. In other words, investors are paying not only for this year's earnings but also for future earnings.

When you compare the forward P/E ratio to the long-term earnings growth rate, you determine the **P/E-to-growth ratio**, or the **PEG ratio**. For example, a stock selling at a forward 15 P/E ratio for a company that is expected to achieve long-term earnings growth of 15 percent per year would have a PEG ratio of 1.0. The PEG ratio is helpful because investors can compare the valuations of companies that are growing at different rates.

Price/book value per share. Book value is a company's assets less its liabilities. This is similar to an individual looking at their net worth. Book value per share is the total book value of the company divided by the number of shares outstanding. If a company has intangible assets, such as patents, these could also be deducted from book value to determine tangible book value. The **price/book value ratio**, or **price/book ratio**, illustrates how much an investor is willing to pay for one share of the company's book value.

For example, a company has a book value of $50 million and 5 million shares outstanding. Book value per share is $50,000,000/5,000,000, or $10 per share. If a stock selling for $20 has a book value per share of $10, the price/book ratio is $20/$10 or 2x. Another way to say this is that the stock is selling for two times book value. Over time, the value of a company's plant and equipment (which are assets) is reduced by depreciation, or writing down the value of long-lived assets. If a company has a lot of old equipment, the book value is lower because the equipment has been written down over time.

Dividend yield. Dividends are distributions of earnings to equity shareholders. Remember that the dividend yield is the dividend per share divided by the price of a share of stock. If you buy one share of stock for $50 and that share pays a $1 dividend, then the dividend yield is $1 divided by $50, or 2 percent. Companies don't distribute all earnings, because they need to keep capital on hand to fund operations and expansion. The earnings that are not distributed are called **retained earnings** and increase the value of the company. The **dividend payout ratio** is dividends per share divided by earnings per share. This ratio shows the proportion of earnings that are paid out to shareholders through dividends.

Dividends are an important consideration for a number of reasons. Dividends are a significant component of total return. Remember that total return on an investment is the increase or decrease in the value of the asset plus dividends or income earned while you hold the investment.

Dividends are more than a distribution, however. They are an indication of a company's financial health. A company's ability to pay a dividend signals that the business is doing well. The stocks of companies that increase dividend payouts from time to time tend to perform well over the long run. In order to increase dividends, a management team must be confident in the company's ability to generate profits today and going forward. In contrast, reducing or eliminating a dividend is a very bad sign and will cause the value of a stock to fall significantly. Because of the importance placed on dividends by investors, management teams do not raise dividends unless they are very confident that they can continue to pay them going forward.

Getting Paid to Wait

With dividend-paying stocks, you earn income as you wait for a stock to appreciate. Dividends are an important component of the total return.

Rather than receiving a cash payment, you can reinvest your dividends back into company stock. Many companies have a **dividend reinvestment plan**, or **DRIP**, through which employees can buy shares directly from the company without having to pay a commission. A DRIP is similar to an automatic savings plan, in that you are building your nest egg and don't really miss the money. At the same time, however, you will have to pay taxes on the dividends. Reinvesting also affects the cost basis, so make sure you keep good records.

TYPES OF STOCKS OR EQUITIES

Domestic stocks are issued by US companies; international stocks are issued by international companies. When looking at a multinational company, or a company that does business in many countries, consider where the business actually makes its money. If a company is based in the United States yet most of its sales are generated overseas, it should be considered an international company. Currency fluctuations have an impact on the value of international stocks—in terms of corporate earnings, the value of the stock, and the dividends earned while you are holding the investment.

There are three main types of international stocks based on the characteristics of the geographic region where the issuing company is located: **developed market stocks, emerging market stocks,** and **frontier market stocks**. Examples of countries from the different types of geographic regions are highlighted in figure 6.2.

Developed markets
- Germany
- France
- United Kingdom
- Japan
- Australia

Emerging markets
- China
- Brazil
- South Korea
- Mexico
- Thailand

Frontier markets
- Kenya
- Vietnam
- Argentina
- Croatia
- Slovenia

Source: MSCI.

Figure 6.2. Examples of geographic markets.

There are important differences among the three types of geographic regions:

- Stocks from developed economies outside the United States often face many of the same opportunities and risks that domestic stocks do. A major difference, however, is the effect of currency fluctuations. Currency fluctuations have an impact on the value of the stock and dividends received, yet they also have an impact on a foreign company's underlying business. Appreciation in the local currency gives international companies more buying power, but it can also make their goods relatively more expensive for foreigners.

- Emerging market stocks are correlated to US domestic stocks in some ways but not in others. Emerging economies are less stable but grow much faster than developed economies. Because emerging markets look to the United States and developed markets for investment dollars, emerging market stocks are affected by what happens in the United States and in other developed countries. Emerging economies are building infrastructure, so commodity prices are also a consideration, as is geopolitical risk.

- A lesser developed emerging market is referred to as a frontier market. The values of stocks from frontier markets are affected by commodity prices, international funding sources, and geopolitical risk. These economies have greater growth prospects than emerging markets. There is also less economic stability in these regions, however, and some frontier stocks can be quite illiquid.

Other Types of Investable Assets

Some investable assets are more specialized and are used less frequently by retail investors. Even though you are more likely to focus on stocks and bonds when you invest, it is a good idea to be familiar with other asset classes. Remember the financial truth that everything is related. Just like your financial decisions, financial markets are interconnected. Also, your needs and circumstances will change over time. What might not be appropriate today might make sense tomorrow.

Derivatives

Derivatives are a type of investment in which the value is derived from something else. The value of a derivative may depend on changes in the price of a stock, the price of an agricultural product, interest rates, or the exchange rate for a foreign currency. Derivatives are used to reduce risk associated with these fluctuations. Investors can trade derivatives as a way to speculate about the direction of interest rates, exchange rates, or the prices of different types of assets, such as stocks or commodities.

An **option** is a common type of derivative. **Calls** and **puts** provide an investor with the opportunity to buy (call) or sell (put) something in the future at a specific price for a certain period. The specific price is called the **strike price**. An investor pays a premium to acquire the option. With an option, the investor decides whether to buy or sell something—a stock, an agricultural product, or foreign currency, which is called **exercising the option**.

An option is **in the money** if exercising the option results in a profit. For example, a call option is in the money if the price of a stock rises above the option's strike price. In this case, exercising the option makes sense because you will make a profit. If the price of the stock falls below a put option's strike price, the put option is in the money. Exercising the put makes sense because you will make a profit. For an **out of the money** option, exercising the option would result in a loss. If an option is not exercised, it expires worthless, and you lose the premium paid.

Options can protect the value of your investments by reducing the downside risk. If you work for a company and own company stock, you can use options to reduce the risk of a decline in the stock price. For example, if you buy a put option, you can sell the stock at a fixed price or establish a floor for the value of your company stock.

Futures contracts are another type of derivative. Whereas an option gives you the opportunity to buy or sell something in the future, a futures contract requires you to buy or sell something in the future. Futures contracts are bought or sold by investors, with an exchange acting as a clearinghouse. Futures contracts are common in agriculture, and enable farmers to lock in prices for their crops. You will also see futures used to hedge or reduce the risk associated with currency or interest rate fluctuations.

Counterparty risk is an important consideration for investors. **Counterparty risk** is the risk that another party will default or not honor an agreement. Because options and futures are traded on an exchange, the exchange acts as an intermediary and helps to minimize counterparty risk.

Master Limited Partnerships, or MLPs

Many energy infrastructure and natural resource companies, such as pipeline or timber companies, are structured as **master limited partnerships**, or **MLPs**. Partnerships are taxed differently than traditional companies. Traditional corporations, which are called C corporations for tax purposes, pay taxes on their income, and then investors pay taxes on the portion of income they receive as dividends. The income distributed as dividends is actually taxed twice: first at the corporate level and second as a dividend.

MLPs involve specific tax and accounting considerations. For MLPs or any partnership, earnings are not taxed at the entity level, and they flow directly through to the partners. The income earned by an MLP is taxed only once. Instead of receiving a 1099 at the end of the year, investors receive a K-1, showing their share of income, gains, and losses.

There is a distinction between the income reported on a K-1 and the distributions received by investors. MLP investors receive distributions, not dividends. Some expenses incurred by natural resource and energy infrastructure companies are noncash. If a pipeline company records depreciation on a piece of equipment, that expense does not represent an actual cash outlay but does reduce net income. Each year, the investor pays taxes on the portion of the distribution that represents net income, as shown on the K-1. The rest of the distribution is tax deferred. It is considered a return of capital and reduces the cost basis. When the investor sells the investment, he or she pays two types of taxes: taxes on the return of capital at ordinary income tax rates, and capital gains taxes if the value of the investment exceeds the cost basis.

Investors may find investing directly in an MLP complicated. MLP funds, however, are structured like a traditional company, or a C corporation. An MLP fund pays taxes at the corporate level, which results in an extra layer of taxation. For an MLP fund, the tax reporting is much simpler, because investors receive a 1099 instead of a K-1.

Although from a tax-reporting perspective, investing in MLP funds is less complicated than directly investing in an MLP, make sure you understand how MLP funds are structured before investing in them. Some MLP funds are closed-end funds that use leverage, or borrow, to enhance returns. I prefer funds that do not use leverage.

Real Estate Investment Trusts, or REITs

Real estate investment trusts, or **REITs**, are funds comprising real estate holdings. A REIT specializes in one type of real estate holding, such as apartment buildings, regional malls, or office buildings. REITs are required to pay out at least 90 percent of taxable net income each year. Distributions are a combination of ordinary income, capital gains, and return of capital, which affects the cost basis. Each year, you pay taxes on the ordinary income and on capital gains. REIT distributions are nonqualified. Like MLPs, REITs can incur noncash expenses, such as depreciation. As a result, the dividends distributed on a REIT could exceed the income earned for a particular year. In those cases, the difference is considered a return of capital. The return of capital reduces your cost basis in the REIT, which will have an impact on the capital gains owed when you sell the investment.

Private Capital

Private capital represents equity investments in private—not publicly traded—companies. Most private capital investments are through funds. Because of high minimum investment requirements, private capital investors are often institutions (pensions, foundations, or endowments) and very high net worth individuals. Private capital funds require a lengthy, multiyear commitment.

There are two main types of private capital funds. **Venture capital funds** invest in early stage companies—rapidly growing start-up companies that are usually not yet profitable. **Private equity funds** also invest in companies that are growing but are more established or beyond the start-up stage. Private equity investments help companies grow their existing business, and the money may also be used to acquire other businesses to expand the platform.

Alternative Assets

Alternative assets have a unique role in an asset allocation. Compared with stocks and bonds, alternative assets have a low correlation to the financial markets. Having an allocation to alternative assets helps reduce the volatility for your total pool of investable assets. In particular, **hedge funds** aim for a low correlation to stock and bond markets in order to provide protection, or a hedge, for your other investments.

One key feature of hedge funds is that they may **sell short**, or **short**, investments. A hedge fund manager sells short when he or she believes that a stock, bond, or other investment will decline in value. For example, a manager borrows stock and sells it to another investor, and then purchases it later at a (hoped-for) lower price. The ability to buy investments and sell others short can offset some of the downside in the market. Buying some investments, or **being long**, and shorting others is called a **long/short strategy**. A portfolio where some holdings do well when the market rises (the long positions) and others do well when the market falls (the shorts) usually results in lower volatility relative to other asset classes.

In contrast to other types of investments, hedge funds focus on absolute return rather than on relative return. For most investments, performance is evaluated on the basis of relative return, or how well an investment performed relative to a market index. In contrast, absolute return focuses on a target return, such as 8 percent to 10 percent.

Like private capital funds, the investment minimums for hedge funds are usually very high. Investing in a fund of funds is an easy way to get exposure to a number of different hedge funds and to invest a lower dollar amount. Managers of a fund of funds adjust the allocation to different types of hedge funds and to different hedge fund firms. In general, hedge fund fees are high compared with other types of investments, and funds of funds add an extra layer on top of the already high fees.

Commodities and Currencies

Investing in commodities, such as metals, energy, and agricultural products, can provide a hedge against inflation. In an inflationary environment, the cost of commodities will rise, and investments in commodities will increase in value. Investing in currencies, such as the British pound, the euro, or the Japanese yen, adds international exposure and diversification to your portfolio. Individual investors often use currencies in specific circumstances, such as to provide a hedge against currency fluctuations for a specific international investment.

CHAPTER 7

Types of Investment Structures: Ways to Invest

J UST AS THERE are many types of investable assets, there are many ways to invest. Let's review the most common methods.

Investable Assets *What to Invest In*	Investment Structures *Ways to Invest*	Investment Accounts *Why to Invest*
• Cash and money market • Bonds • Equities • Derivatives • Master limited partnerships (MLPs) • Real estate investment trusts (REITs) • Private capital • Alternative assets • Commodities and currencies	• Individual account • Mutual funds • Index funds • Exchange traded funds (ETFs) • Exchange traded notes (ETNs) • Target date funds	• Taxable • 401(k) and 403(b) • IRA • Roth IRA and 401(k) • Annuities • 529 plans
Fundamental Investing Concepts		

Figure 7.1. Investment structures.

Individual Accounts

People can invest in bonds, stocks, or other securities by working with a professional at a brokerage firm. An individual account with a broker or financial adviser is also known as a **separate account**. You can also manage a separate account by yourself. Many brokerage firms operate online platforms and have physical branches located across the United States. Investors pay a commission for each trade, but firms like these also offer funds without commissions, loads, or transaction fees.

Whether you invest on your own or with a broker, you have the option of using margin in an attempt to increase returns. **Margin accounts** allow investors to borrow against their holdings. The investable assets in the account are collateral for a **margin loan**. The money borrowed with a margin loan enables an investor to put more money to work. Loans, or leverage, can enhance returns, but they also increase risk significantly.

For example, if a stock you own that is used as collateral for a margin loan declines in value, you will face a margin call. With a **margin call**, you will need to put up cash as additional collateral for the margin loan.

Although hedge funds do it, selling stocks short in an individual account is a risky way to enhance returns. Remember that selling a stock short, or shorting a stock, means that you borrow stock and sell it to another investor. You will buy the stock at a later time at what you hope will be a lower price. Selling short can be risky because of the unlimited downside risk. If you buy a stock, the most you can lose is the price paid for it. There is no limit, however, to how high a stock might go. For example, if you sell short stock in a company and another company decides to acquire the company that you are shorting, the stock can rise significantly on the day that the deal is announced. If you have sold short a stock that surges in value quickly, your losses will be large.

Sometimes it is difficult to create a diversified portfolio if you don't have a significant amount of money to invest. In a portfolio, having at least twenty to twenty-five holdings, or **positions**, is preferable. If you do not have enough money to invest in twenty to twenty-five different stocks or bonds, consider an investment fund.

Many different types of funds are discussed in this chapter. Detailed information about funds is available in a fund's prospectus, which can be cumbersome and quite technical. Financial firms are required to provide investors with essential information in the numerous disclosures that accompany marketing materials. The discussion here should help you figure out what information is most important for your investment decisions.

Mutual Funds

Mutual funds offered by asset management firms are the most common type of investment fund. There are different structures and styles of mutual funds. The two main structures are called "open-end" and "closed-end." We will also cover the two main investing approaches for mutual funds—active and passive.

Open-End Mutual Funds

In an **open-end mutual fund**, individuals buy shares directly from the asset management company. The fund's **portfolio manager**, or **PM**, invests money provided by investors who have bought shares in the fund. Asset management firms sell as many shares as investors want to buy. The money going into open-end mutual funds is called an **inflow**. The money coming out of open-end mutual funds is an **outflow**, or **redemption**.

The total amount of money in a mutual fund is called **assets under management**, or **AUM**.

Open-end mutual fund shares are priced at the **net asset value**, or **NAV**, at the end of each trading day. Per share NAV is the value of the fund's assets minus its liabilities divided by the number of shares outstanding. If the value of the portfolio holdings rises or falls during the trading day, the NAV rises or falls. Unlike other types of investable assets, you can invest in an open-end mutual fund only at the end of the trading day. Likewise, if you want to sell, or redeem, your shares in an open-end fund, you redeem directly from the fund manager at NAV or sell back your shares to the fund manager at the end of the day.

Although open-end funds can sell an unlimited number of shares to investors, an asset management company might close a fund if the amount of money in the fund grows too large. For a stock fund with substantial AUM, the portfolio manager will need to buy or sell large blocks of stock, which can pose problems. If buy or sell orders are substantial compared to a stock's normal daily trading volume, the large trades can have an impact on the stock's price, or **move the market**.

Portfolio managers are more likely to close small-cap and microcap funds than they are to close large-cap funds because small and microcap companies have fewer shares outstanding. In addition, senior management and employees of a small-cap or microcap company, or **insiders**, might own a large proportion of the stock. Large insider ownership means that there is less stock available to outside investors, or less **float**. Sometimes a mutual fund is closed to new investors, but existing investors can continue to put money in the fund.

Mutual funds carry the risk of **embedded capital gains**. When you invest in a mutual fund, you own a share in a pool of assets. You do not own individual assets within that pool.

This may seem like a subtle distinction, but it is important. On the day that you invest in a mutual fund, your share in the pool of assets could include holdings that have appreciated since the fund manager originally bought them and are valued above cost. You don't get the benefit of that appreciation, however, because you are investing at today's NAV.

For mutual funds, capital gains are realized when the portfolio manager makes a distribution. The manager distributes a certain amount per share in cash to all shareholders of record as of a particular date, thus reducing the level of embedded capital gains in the fund.

Mutual funds are not as tax efficient as separate, or individually managed, accounts. Table 7.1 uses a hypothetical example

TABLE 7.1. Risk of embedded capital gains for mutual funds.

Invest $1,000 in a Fund Today
Own 5 Percent of the $20,000 AUM Fund with an Embedded Capital Gain

Fund	Cost Basis	Value	Gain/(Loss)
100 Stock A	$35x100=$3,500	$45x100=$4,500	$1,000
100 Stock B	$30x100=$3,000	$25x100=$2,500	($500)
100 Stock C	$50x100=$5,000	$40x100=$4,000	($1,000)
100 Stock D	$60x100=$6,000	$75x100=$7,500	$1,500
Cash	$1,500	$1,500	$0
Totals	$19,000	$20,000	$1,000

Invest $1,000 in a Separate Account Today
No Embedded Capital Gain

Account	Cost Basis	Value	Gain/(Loss)
5 Stock A	$45x5=$225	$45x5=$225	$0
5 Stock B	$25x5=$125	$25x5=$125	$0
5 Stock C	$40x5=$200	$40x5=$200	$0
5 Stock D	$75x5=$375	$75x5=$375	$0
Cash	$75	$75	$0
Totals	$1,000	$1,000	$0

to illustrate the difference between investing $1,000 today in a mutual fund and $1,000 today in a separate account.

For the fund, the embedded capital gains are present the day that you invest. Even though you did not benefit from the increased value of the underlying holdings, you are responsible for the capital gains, which could be distributed (and taxable) at any point in time. In a separate account, however, there are no embedded capital gains. You deposit money in the account and begin to make investments. No preexisting holdings have appreciated or have embedded capital gains.

You can analyze the potential for embedded capital gains. Websites such as Morningstar provide an estimate of embedded capital gains for a mutual fund. Morningstar and the fund manager's website will provide a history of distributions from a fund, and you can look up a manager's record of capital gains distributions. Investigate how recently distributions have occurred, as well has how much has been distributed and at what times of year. If a fund appreciates significantly during the year, the likelihood of a capital gains distribution increases. Avoid investing in a mutual fund late in the calendar year because you could be hit with a capital gains distribution and tax bill soon thereafter.

Closed-End Funds

Closed-end funds are not as common as open-end funds. Closed-end funds usually comprise income-producing investments, such as bonds or stocks with high dividends. These funds are favored by investors seeking current income. Unlike an open-end fund, which can continue to sell shares to investors, a closed-end fund raises money once, and the number of shares is fixed. There is an initial offering for a closed-end fund just like for a stock or bond. The initial offering involves underwriting fees and commissions. Some investors wait until after the initial offering to invest in a closed-end fund, so as to avoid paying up-front underwriting fees and commissions.

Closed-end fund valuations are driven by supply and demand, not daily NAV. Closed-end funds usually trade at a premium or a discount to NAV. If an investor wants to exit a closed-end fund, he or she must sell to another investor. This is unlike open-end funds, where investors redeem directly from the asset management company at NAV or sell back their shares at today's valuation. Open-end funds trade at the end of the day, whereas closed-end funds trade throughout the day.

Actively Managed Mutual Funds

For **actively managed funds**, a portfolio manager researches and chooses the holdings, or securities, that he or she finds the most attractive. The portfolio manager also continues to evaluate existing holdings to see if they should remain in the fund. Actively managed funds invest in stocks, bonds, and other types of securities. When researching potential holdings for a stock fund, for example, the portfolio manager looks at a company's earnings, cash flow, and balance sheet. He or she also looks at factors such as product quality, market share, new product pipelines, and the strength of the management team. In other words, the portfolio manager analyzes a company's fundamental attributes, or its **fundamentals**, along with the stock's valuation, to determine whether to make an investment or to continue to hold the stock in the portfolio. Buying and selling portfolio holdings is called **portfolio turnover**. The level of turnover varies by manager. In addition to increased transaction costs, high portfolio turnover is less tax efficient because of capital gains.

With an actively managed fund, the portfolio manager tries to generate alpha or a return that is better than the index, or benchmark. For equities, active managers are sometimes referred to as "stock pickers." A **stock picker's market** is when the quality of a company's fundamental attributes drives the demand for and performance of stocks. This is also called a "fundamentally driven market." In a stock picker's market, quality is a differentiating factor, and research is important. The same is true for bonds. Doing in-depth research regarding the quality and valuation of a bond is essential for good investment performance in fundamentally driven markets.

In hot markets, or **momentum-driven markets**, there is less emphasis on research and on analyzing an investment's fundamental attributes. In a momentum-driven market, valuations rise across the board. As the saying goes, "A rising tide lifts all boats." Sometimes when the market rises significantly, even lower-quality securities do well. In fact, lower-quality stocks can sometimes appreciate more rapidly than higher-quality securities in a momentum-driven market. For example, when demand for stocks is strong, some lower-quality stocks may appear to be a relative bargain, especially when there is a lot of enthusiasm for a particular sector. Investors may underestimate the risk associated with lower-quality stocks when they see them as more attractively valued opportunities. Lower-quality stocks may be a bargain for a very good reason—volatile earnings, higher debt, lower profit margins, or a weak management team. Remember, value depends on what someone is willing to pay for an asset, not on the quality of the asset. It does not matter if it is a stock picker's market or a momentum-driven market, value is subjective, not objective.

For actively managed stock mutual funds, managers usually have a style or market-cap specialization. With a market-cap specialization, managers invest only in companies of a particular size, such as large-cap or small-cap companies. These size restrictions usually apply only to the initial investment. For example, a small-cap portfolio manager may invest only in companies with a market capitalization of less than $2 billion. If the portfolio manager is a good stock picker, the stocks will appreciate and exceed the $2 billion threshold. Portfolio managers will probably not sell these stocks right away even though the stocks have exceeded the small-cap definition. This is called "letting your winners run."

In addition to market-cap specialization, active managers may focus on a certain investing style. For stock funds, there are two main active management styles. **Growth managers** invest in companies with strong earnings growth. They look at the long-term earnings growth rate, the forward P/E ratio, and the PEG ratio, in addition to the quality of the earnings and the strength of the balance sheet. Growth stock managers tend to invest in stocks with greater than expected earnings growth and, consequently, higher price/earnings multiples. The key is to find stocks that will increase earnings faster than expected. Growth stock portfolios often include companies in fast-growing industries, such as technology, telecommunications, and biotech.

> ### Growth at a Reasonable Price, or GARP
>
> Some growth managers look for companies that are increasing earnings but also have an attractive valuation. Their portfolios are more likely to hold stable growers than high-flying stocks with lofty valuations.

In contrast to growth managers, **value managers** focus primarily on a stock's valuation. Value managers invest in companies that are attractively valued or are trading at a discount to what the portfolio manager thinks the company's underlying assets are worth. Value managers look for lower P/Es, lower price/book ratios, and attractive dividend yields. Utilities pay relatively high dividends and are often included in value portfolios. Value managers tend to prefer stable stocks that can perform well in strong or weak economic environments—these are also known as **defensive stocks**. Utilities and companies that produce consumer staples, such as soap and toothpaste, are examples of defensive stocks.

Some value managers focus on out-of-favor companies and industries or turnaround situations. A company could face a short-term issue, such as a temporary shortage in a raw material that is used in production or issues related to the weather that have a negative impact on the business. These are examples of short-term factors that should not affect the long-term prospects for a company. Value managers with a long-term orientation are willing to invest in stocks and hold onto them, or to "weather the storm."

Passive, or Index, Funds

Index funds are a type of mutual fund that replicates the performance of an index. Examples of common indices are:

- S&P 500 for large-cap stocks
- Russell 2000 for small-cap stocks
- MSCI EAFE for international stocks
- Wilshire 5000 for the total stock market
- Barclays US Aggregate for bonds

Because the composition of these funds is based on an index rather than on a portfolio manager choosing stocks or bonds, these funds are called **passive investments**. Compared with actively managed funds, index funds are lower-cost alternatives. Portfolio turnover and transaction costs are lower than for actively managed funds. If an actively managed fund makes a lot of trades, or has high portfolio turnover, transaction costs will be high. When costs are high, managers must charge high fees. In addition, because the composition of an index fund is based on an index, the portfolio manager does not need to research new portfolio ideas. This reduces the expenses associated with managing the fund. For index funds, dividends and interest income from underlying holdings are reinvested into the fund. Distributions are made periodically, usually on a quarterly basis. Index funds are a type of mutual fund, so investors can buy or sell shares only at the end of the day.

Index funds include all the investments in the index, but the amount of each investment varies, depending on how the fund is **weighted**. Most stock index funds are market-cap weighted rather than equal weighted. With a market-cap weighted fund, there is a greater weighting, or emphasis, on the largest-cap companies in the index. A market-cap weighted index will earn higher returns than an equal weighted fund when the largest-cap stocks are performing relatively better than smaller-cap stocks.

At the same time, however, strong performance for large-cap stocks could increase the risk for market-cap weighted funds. If larger-cap stocks are in favor and rise significantly, they will represent an ever-larger proportion of a market-weighted index fund. Therefore, the index fund will have a greater allocation of stocks that have appreciated considerably and could be considered overvalued.

With an equal weighted fund, every stock or bond has the same weight. Compared with a market-cap weighted fund, relatively more emphasis is placed on smaller- and midcap holdings. Equal weighted index funds will perform better than market-cap weighted indexes when the stocks of smaller and midsize companies are appreciating more than the shares of larger-cap companies.

A market-cap weighted fund could skew the true exposure to a sector or region. As an illustration, the MSCI Emerging Market Index is a market-cap weighted index. Because Samsung Electronics is based in South Korea, it is considered an emerging markets stock. Not surprisingly, it is one of the largest holdings in the emerging markets index. Most people think of Samsung as a global brand, however, not as a company from an emerging market.

Fundamental weighted index funds adjust the weighting of the index holdings based on factors such as growth in sales, the dividend yield, and the amount of debt, or leverage, on the company's balance sheet. Relative to a regular market-cap or equal cap weighted index, fundamental indices can have higher portfolio turnover, which means higher transaction costs and fees.

Exchange Traded Funds, or ETFs

Exchange traded funds, or **ETFs**, are similar to index funds in that they replicate the performance of an index or sector of the economy or the market. There are several distinctions, however. For ETFs, a major brokerage firm, known as an authorized participant, creates a basket of securities. The authorized participant sells shares of the ETF to investors. ETFs trade throughout the day, not just at the end of the day, like a mutual fund. The funds have lower management fees than index funds do. In some cases, you will pay a commission when you invest in an ETF. If you are investing in ETFs regularly through an automatic savings plan, be careful because the commissions can add up. For mutual funds, you pay based on a percentage of assets, not on how many transactions you make. Some brokerage firms offer no-commission ETFs.

Unlike an index fund, ETFs accumulate dividends and interest income from the underlying holdings and make regular distributions rather than reinvesting the income. Compared with mutual funds, ETFs are more tax efficient. Mutual funds distribute capital gains to all shareholders when the manager makes the distribution. An investor realizes a capital gain on an

ETF when the investor sells shares or units. Sometimes mutual funds can have high minimums for investment; ETFs do not.

Alternative weightings ETFs provide specific exposures to market sectors or strategies. Some focus on a fundamental metric, such as dividend yield or price-to-book value ratio.

Managed ETF portfolios are made up of various ETFs. These portfolios provide access to different types of asset classes and markets, or they can represent a specific investment strategy. Managed ETFs are actively managed rather than passive portfolios. Strategists design the portfolios, make allocation decisions across ETFs, and reallocate, or rebalance, from time to time. Managed portfolios are commonly used for online wealth and retirement planning programs, and many financial advisers also use them. Fees are closer to mutual fund fees than to ETF fees, because managed ETFs require active management. Because managed ETFs are relatively new, some managers have short track records. Make sure that an ETF's performance track record is compliant with Global Investment Performance Standards, or GIPS, from the CFA Institute. Confirm whether the performance record is actual or hypothetical.

The risks associated with ETFs depend on the structure and composition of the fund. **Physical ETFs** invest in actual underlying assets, and the authorized agent creates a basket of securities. In contrast, **synthetic ETFs** use derivatives to mimic the performance of an index or sector. The use of derivatives for an ETF can be riskier than investing in underlying assets. Synthetic ETFs are more common in Europe than in the United States because of regulatory and tax differences. Be careful of ETFs that are made up of assets that are not liquid. These assets can become even less liquid in the event of financial turmoil.

Exchange traded notes, or **ETNs**, are a type of unsecured debt security. ETNs do not pay interest like a bond; they generate a return based on the performance of an index. With an

ETN, you don't own a stake in a portfolio of assets. The issuer is usually a bank or other financial institution. The principal of the note is neither protected nor guaranteed. There is counterparty risk, so check the creditworthiness of the issuer. ETNs can trade on exchanges, and fees are usually higher for ETNs than for ETFs. Different types of ETNs are taxed differently, so confirm how income on the investment is taxed.

Target date funds change the allocation across various asset classes as retirement approaches. The funds automatically rebalance and change the allocation periodically to meet targets. Allocations are based on how asset classes have performed historically. The automatic rebalancing can be appealing, but investors need to monitor the allocation and performance closely and on a regular basis. Target date fund fees are often fairly high.

Depending on market conditions as your retirement draws near, traditionally safe asset classes may not be as safe. Bonds have appreciated considerably in recent years and may not be as safe an asset class as they were in the past. You should never think of investing as a "set it and forget it" exercise. You may have a different risk tolerance or different needs than other people. If target date funds are appealing, I favor using them for only a portion of your asset allocation.

CHAPTER 8

Types of Investment Accounts: Why to Invest

INVESTMENTS RESIDE in various types of accounts that serve different purposes. Investment accounts may be designed to save for retirement, college, or other general purposes. In this

Investable Assets *What to Invest In*	Investment Structures *Ways to Invest*	Investment Accounts *Why to Invest*
• Cash and money market • Bonds • Equities • Derivatives • Master limited partnerships (MLPs) • Real estate investment trusts (REITs) • Private capital • Alternative assets • Commodities and currencies	• Individual account • Mutual funds • Index funds • Exchange traded funds (ETFs) • Exchange traded notes (ETNs) • Target date funds	• Taxable • 401(k) and 403(b) • IRA • Roth IRA and 401(k) • Annuities • 529 plans

Fundamental Investing Concepts

Figure 8.1. Investment accounts.

chapter, we will cover taxable accounts, retirement accounts, annuities, and college savings accounts.

With investment accounts, it is important to distinguish whether they are taxable, tax deferred, or tax advantaged. To encourage individuals to save for retirement or a college education, the US government created types of investment accounts that either defer the taxes owed (tax deferred) or grow tax free (tax advantaged). All other types of investment accounts are considered taxable accounts.

Taxable Accounts

Although there are no tax benefits, taxable accounts are more liquid and more flexible than tax-deferred or tax-advantaged accounts. Investors can gain access to funds without penalties like those that exist for the other types of accounts. There are several things to keep in mind or track for taxable accounts.

Dividends and Interest

Interest and nonqualified dividends are taxed at the ordinary income rate, and qualified dividends are taxed at a lower rate. (Remember that the ordinary income rate is the same rate that you pay on your wages or salary.) There are, however, some exceptions:

- For some types of municipal bonds, interest is not subject to federal income taxes or taxes at the state or local level if the bond is issued by the state or municipality where you reside.
- Interest on a municipal bond is taxable if the bond is within a mutual fund.
- Interest on US government bonds is not taxable at the state and local level but is taxable at the federal level.

When deciding among corporate, government, and municipal bonds, you can compute a tax-equivalent yield to compare different options. The **tax-equivalent yield** is the yield on a tax-exempt bond divided by 1 minus your tax rate. This formula allows you to compare two options that are taxed differently:

tax-exempt bond yield ÷ (1 – your tax rate) = tax-equivalent yield

Capital Gains and Losses

Remember that there is a difference in the taxation of short-term capital gains for an investment held one year or less and long-term capital gains for an investment held for more than one year. Short-term capital gains are taxed at the same rate as ordinary income. Long-term capital gains are taxed at rates of up to 20.0 percent. Also remember that you can offset investment gains with losses in a given year. You can also carry forward losses and use them in subsequent years to offset future capital gains. Make sure that you do not buy back a stock within 30 days of selling it, or it will be a wash sale; you cannot realize a loss from a wash sale.

Cost Basis

As you monitor your investments, don't forget to track factors that affect the cost basis and taxation. Both stock splits and reinvested dividends have an impact on cost basis. If you inherit an investment, the cost basis **steps up** in most cases. With inherited securities, the cost basis is not what the person originally paid. Instead the cost basis steps up or is equal to the security's fair market value on the date of death or on an alternative valuation date used for estate tax purposes. When you sell inherited securities, all capital gains are considered long-term and are taxed at the lower rate.

Retirement Accounts

There are many ways to save for retirement. Because fewer and fewer Americans have traditional pension plans, I focus here on other types of retirement accounts—401(k)s, 403(b)s, IRAs, Roth IRAs, and Roth 401(k)s. These accounts all have tax benefits, which are discussed in each section.

401(k) and 403(b) Accounts

A common type of retirement account is a 401(k) plan offered by an employer. With a **401(k) plan**, you invest pretax dollars. Money comes out of your paycheck before it is taxed as income and goes straight into an account. The dollars invested grow tax deferred. When you retire, you pay taxes on withdrawals. This account benefits you because, in retirement, you will no longer be working or you may be working part-time. Your income and your tax bracket may be lower in retirement than during your working years so you would pay less taxes than when you are working full-time.

Some companies offer to match 401(k) contributions up to a specific amount. A corporate match is free money, and it is essential that you take full advantage of these opportunities. Not only is the match free, but saving this way will help you ramp up your retirement savings.

A **403(b) plan** is like a 401(k) plan, but it is for employees of the government and nonprofit organizations. In the past, 403(b) accounts could invest only in annuities. Now these plans have more investment options. Annuities can have high fees, which has a negative impact on the growth of your savings.

IRAs

Individual retirement accounts, or **IRAs**, are funded with pretax dollars. These accounts grow tax deferred like a 401(k) does, and you pay taxes when you withdraw the money upon retirement. But there are restrictions on contributions, depending on your age, income level, and whether you are eligible for a retirement plan at work. Currently, individuals are allowed to put away $5,500 in an IRA each year (or $6,500 if they are age fifty or older.) A **simplified employee pension plan**, or **SEP plan**, is an option for self-employed people or those who work at small firms. These are also called **SEP IRAs**.

When you leave a job or retire, you can roll over your 401(k) or 403(b) into an IRA. You will probably have a variety of jobs during your lifetime. By rolling over your 401(k) or 403(b) into an IRA, you will put all your money in one pool, making it much easier to analyze your retirement savings. Remember that it is important to take a comprehensive view of your financial life. Consolidating your retirement accounts into one pool is easier to monitor.

Roth IRAs and Roth 401(k)s

In contrast to traditional IRAs and 401(k)s, **Roth IRAs** and **Roth 401(k)s** are funded with after-tax dollars. The contributions do not reduce your taxable income. In other words, you make contributions to a Roth from your take-home pay after it has been taxed. Roth retirement accounts grow tax free. Moreover, you do not pay taxes on withdrawals if the account has been open for at least five years. A Roth is an example of a tax-advantaged account. Some employers offer Roth 401(k) plans. Contributions to Roth IRAs are limited to those who earn below a threshold amount, whereas contributions to Roth 401(k)s are not. Currently, the IRS limits Roth IRA contributions to those making less than $135,000 or $199,000 if married.

It is possible to convert a 401(k), 403(b), or IRA into a Roth IRA. With a Roth conversion, you pay taxes when converting the account. There are several things to consider if you are thinking of converting to a Roth IRA. It is a good option for those who think that their marginal tax rate will be higher when they retire. The further away you are from retirement, the greater the advantage of a Roth IRA. Don't convert to a Roth IRA if you need to borrow money from the account to pay the taxes due upon conversion. If you convert to a Roth IRA following a period of significant market appreciation, you will pay a larger tax bill than if you convert when asset values are depressed.

Withdrawing from a Retirement Account

You can begin withdrawing from retirement accounts at age 59½. If you withdraw money from a retirement account before age 59½, you will pay a 10 percent penalty to the IRS in addition to any regular income taxes owed. Certain situations where the penalty does not apply are listed on the IRS's website.

Required minimum distributions, or **RMDs**, are the required minimum amounts that you must withdraw from an IRA each year, beginning at age 70½. RMD tables are available on the IRS's website and are based on life expectancy. If you inherit an IRA from someone who started taking withdrawals, you will be required to take withdrawals regardless of your age, although the RMD is based on your life expectancy, not on that of the person who passed away. There are no RMDs for a Roth IRA, unless the Roth IRA is inherited. For inherited Roth IRAs, consult the IRS website, because the rules can be complex.

Annuities

Annuities are contracts offered by insurance companies and are often used to save for retirement. Annuities provide contract holders a future payment or series of payments, which can be fixed or variable. The growth in the annuity is tax deferred. When you receive the money, you pay taxes on the earnings at ordinary income rates.

There are two main types of annuities. With a fixed annuity, you receive a predetermined return. The return can be a specific amount, or it can be tied to a market index. Fixed annuities are not securities but rather are an insurance product and are regulated by state insurance departments.

With a variable annuity, you choose among investment options and you bear the investment risk. Variable annuities are considered securities and are regulated by the Securities and Exchange Commission (SEC).

Annuities are complex and can be expensive: you may pay an up-front commission to a salesperson and pay administrative fees. There are underlying expenses for the fund options offered through a variable annuity. In addition, you will likely pay a surrender fee to the annuity provider if you withdraw early in the contract. There can be other fees for added benefits, such as a guaranteed minimum return or for mortality risk. If you withdraw money before the age of 59½, you will pay taxes on the income earned plus a 10 percent penalty to the IRS. There are some exceptions, which you can find on the IRS website. Annuities are a contract but not a guarantee. Contracts can be broken, so annuities carry counterparty risk.

For most people, it does not make sense to invest in an annuity within an IRA account, because an annuity already grows tax deferred. Originally, 403(b) plans were required to use annuities. Now 403(b) plans also offer mutual fund options, which usually have much lower fees than annuities. Compared with other options, the various fees associated with annuities can add up.

529 Plans

The most common type of college savings programs is a 529 plan. Assets in a 529 plan grow tax free. Contributions to the plan are not tax deductible at the federal level, but they may be at the state level. Withdrawals are tax free at the federal level as long as the money is used for qualifying expenses. Depending on the state, there can be additional tax benefits for withdrawals.

With a 529, be careful about the timing of tuition and other related payments and the timing of account withdrawals. In addition, confirm which expenses are qualified and which are not. Qualified expenses are primarily tuition, room, board, books, and mandatory fees or equipment required for course-work. Recent tax law changes mean that 529 plans also can be used for K–12 private school tuition. There are penalties for early withdrawals and for withdrawals for uses other than qual-ified expenses. For withdrawals for nonqualified expenses, you will pay taxes on the portion that represents income, or invest-ment earnings. Remember that 529 accounts are funded with after-tax dollars.

Putting Everything to Work

The four chapters in this section have covered a lot of infor-mation about investing. Now that you have gotten organized, have taken an objective look at your finances, and are familiar with some basic concepts, it is time to put your knowledge into practice. You are ready to be more actively involved in manag-ing your financial life.

PART 4

Invest Your Money

You may delay, but time will not.

—BENJAMIN FRANKLIN

Now that you understand some fundamental investing concepts and are familiar with different types of assets, investment structures, and investment accounts, it is time to put your money to work. This section covers how to implement what you have learned and how to better invest your money. You start by figuring out what you will need, and then you figure out how to get there. You will have to ask yourself some tough questions and make some hard decisions. There are various topics to consider: your savings goals, your investment choices, which investing platforms work best for you, and how your investments are performing.

CHAPTER 9

Determine Your Savings Goals: What Are You Investing For? How Much Do You Need?

BEFORE YOU CAN develop an investment strategy, you have to articulate your financial needs and what you expect from your money. You also need to establish your priorities in conjunction with your partner. This chapter will help you get started.

To assess your financial needs, ask yourself the following questions:

- Do you need current income, such as dividends or interest, to support your present lifestyle?
- Are there any impending near-term changes in your life?
- What are your long-term plans? Do you plan to retire in twenty years? Ten years? Any plans to take a sabbatical?
- What about other long-term plans, such as having children, a change in work status, travel, starting a business, purchasing a vacation home?

- Do you have plans to go back to school? Do you want to help your children with college expenses?
- Do you want to support certain charities?
- Are there special factors to consider, such as health issues?
- Do other people rely on you for financial support?
- Do you have children or other family members with special needs?
- Are you interested in and willing to work part-time during retirement?
- Would you like to downsize or possibly relocate in retirement?

Answering these questions will help you evaluate your priorities and needs. Once you have a handle on these, you can start to set savings goals that will help guide your investment strategy. Whatever you are saving for—retirement, college, a vacation home—setting concrete savings goals increases the likelihood that you will achieve what you want.

Time Is Your Friend

Time is your friend in two ways. First, I cannot overemphasize the positive impact that time has on your money. Contributing regularly to retirement and savings plans and starting to contribute early have a dramatic effect on how much you will be able to save. Table 9.1 shows the effect of different savings rates over time. Saving $1,000 or $2,000 per year makes a big difference in the size of your nest egg after thirty years. If you save more than that, the impact is even greater.

Second, different goals have different time horizons. Some are imminent—such as establishing an emergency fund—and some, like retirement, are longer term in nature. Trying to tackle all your savings goals at once is overwhelming and unrealistic. Thinking

TABLE 9.1. Impact of regular savings.

| Assumed return | 7.0 percent |
| Assumed fee | 1.0 percent |

Year	Initial	Year-end balance	Initial and additions	Year-end balance	Initial and additions	Year-end balance
1	$1,000	$1,060	$1,000	$1,060	$2,000	$2,120
2	$0	$1,124	$1,000	$2,184	$2,000	$4,367
3	$0	$1,191	$1,000	$3,375	$2,000	$6,749
4	$0	$1,262	$1,000	$4,637	$2,000	$9,274
5	$0	$1,338	$1,000	$5,975	$2,000	$11,951
6	$0	$1,419	$1,000	$7,394	$2,000	$14,788
7	$0	$1,504	$1,000	$8,897	$2,000	$17,795
8	$0	$1,594	$1,000	$10,491	$2,000	$20,983
9	$0	$1,689	$1,000	$12,181	$2,000	$24,362
10	$0	$1,791	$1,000	$13,972	$2,000	$27,943
11	$0	$1,898	$1,000	$15,870	$2,000	$31,740
12	$0	$2,012	$1,000	$17,882	$2,000	$35,764
13	$0	$2,133	$1,000	$20,015	$2,000	$40,030
14	$0	$2,261	$1,000	$22,276	$2,000	$44,552
15	$0	$2,397	$1,000	$24,673	$2,000	$49,345
16	$0	$2,540	$1,000	$27,213	$2,000	$54,426
17	$0	$2,693	$1,000	$29,906	$2,000	$59,811
18	$0	$2,854	$1,000	$32,760	$2,000	$65,520
19	$0	$3,026	$1,000	$35,786	$2,000	$71,571
20	$0	$3,207	$1,000	$38,993	$2,000	$77,985
21	$0	$3,400	$1,000	$42,392	$2,000	$84,785
22	$0	$3,604	$1,000	$45,996	$2,000	$91,992
23	$0	$3,820	$1,000	$49,816	$2,000	$99,631
24	$0	$4,049	$1,000	$53,865	$2,000	$107,729
25	$0	$4,292	$1,000	$58,156	$2,000	$116,313
26	$0	$4,549	$1,000	$62,706	$2,000	$125,412
27	$0	$4,822	$1,000	$67,528	$2,000	$135,056
28	$0	$5,112	$1,000	$72,640	$2,000	$145,280
29	$0	$5,418	$1,000	$78,058	$2,000	$156,116
30	$0	$5,743	$1,000	$83,802	$2,000	$167,603
		Difference		$78,059		$161,860

Note: Assumes that the initial investment and any additions are made at the beginning of the year.

about time horizons helps you prioritize your goals and use a more methodical and organized approach to working toward them. Table 9.2 shows an example of different goals, different time horizons, and a way to prioritize various financial needs.

The goals and plans listed in table 9.2 are for illustrative purposes only. Remember: everyone's financial needs and goals are unique.

TABLE 9.2. Setting savings goals.

Financial need	Time horizon	Savings goal	Savings plan
Emergency fund	Now	6 months' expenses	$400 per month until reached
Down payment	3 years	20% down	After emergency fund is set up, $500 per month
College	18 years	75% of expenses	After down payment, $200 per month for 529 plan
Retirement	35 years	Multiple of income	Max out your 401(k) Check your multiple each year
Other	Long-term	Supplement retirement	Any extra after other needs are taken care of to put toward retirement

Imminent Need: Emergency Fund

The most immediate savings goal is your emergency fund. Experts recommend that you have an emergency fund sufficient to cover living expenses for at least six months. Emergency funds are vital in case you or your partner lose your job. Make sure that the assets in the emergency fund are very liquid, such as cash in a savings account or in a money market fund.

In some instances, you may need an emergency fund that is bigger than six months of living expenses. You may face hurdles when looking for a new job, such as geographic restrictions or the need for flexibility in terms of travel or work hours.

If you have health issues or a dependent with special needs, your emergency fund should be larger than six months.

If you need to dip into your emergency fund, replenish it as soon as possible. Of course you hope you won't need to dip into your emergency fund again soon, but you never know. Better safe than sorry.

Long-Term Need: Retirement Savings

Saving enough for retirement is the biggest concern for many of us and one of the most important topics addressed in this book. For some people, retirement is a long way off. For others, it is right around the corner. Whatever your timing, there are many unknowns—whether you will work part-time, where you will live, how much money you will need for day-to-day expenses, the state of your health, how long you will live. Many people find the retirement planning process daunting. But it is important to start thinking about the unknowns and variables now, regardless of your age.

You will likely need multiple sources of savings to fund your retirement:

- Most Americans working today do not have a defined benefit pension plan or a traditional pension. The primary sources of retirement funds come from defined contribution pension plans, such as 401(k)s and 403(b)s, and from IRAs (figure 9.1).
- Social Security is a source of retirement funds. You can go to ssa.gov/estimator to estimate your future Social Security benefits. If you can afford to, it is advantageous to delay collecting benefits from age sixty-five to age seventy. The Social Security Administration bases its computations on old mortality tables that project shorter life expectancies than exist today. The benefit payments at seventy reflect this, which means a higher payment than if the computations were based on current life expectancies.
- Another source of retirement funds is personal savings.

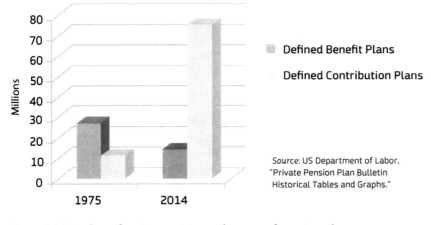

Defined Benefit Plans

Defined Contribution Plans

Source: US Department of Labor,
"Private Pension Plan Bulletin
Historical Tables and Graphs."

Figure 9.1. Number of active participants by type of pension plan.

Retirement savings guidelines can provide you with an estimate of what you need to save. Many financial websites offer retirement calculators. Compare a few guidelines and tools— you may get different answers. With longer-term savings goals, it is difficult to predict your future salary or how much items will cost in the future. Nonetheless, working through this exercise will help you gauge your progress toward your savings goals.

Retirement Calculators

The outputs, or answers, derived from retirement calculators are only as good as the inputs. For income needs during retirement, factor in 70–85 percent of your preretirement salary. But it is challenging to estimate your salary in ten, twenty, or thirty years, so try different scenarios. Some of your expenses in retirement will go down. Work-related expenses, such as commuting, dry cleaning, and eating lunches out, will be reduced after you retire. You will not be making retirement plan contributions. At the same time, some expenses, like leisure travel and health care, will likely go up. You could start with your current expense analysis and normalized cash flow, discussed in chapter 3, and adjust it to reflect anticipated changes in your lifestyle once you retire.

As you work with calculators, be mindful of the difference between income and expenses in today's dollars and income and expenses in the future. To project future expense and income amounts, you need to factor in inflation. Some retirement planning calculators take your current salary and assume an annual increase each year to come up with a preretirement salary. Others allow you to input current expenses, and the calculator will incorporate inflation and provide an estimate of future spending needs. Most calculators adjust inputs for both salary increases and inflation.

Retirement Guidelines

A common guideline is to build a retirement fund that is equal to a multiple of your preretirement income. It is easy to benchmark progress when you use a multiple. Experts suggest striving for a multiple from eight to fifteen times your salary at age sixty-five. If you plan to retire before age sixty-five, or if you have a high income and a high standard of living, aim for the upper end of the range.

No matter which method you use to compute your retirement savings goal, you need to chart progress over time. Using a multiple can help you understand whether you are on track. Compare your current retirement savings balance with your current salary to assess your progress. Computing the multiple based on your current salary will help you determine whether you need to ramp up savings.

Unless you are facing an emergency, do not borrow from your retirement account—if you do, you will miss the growth opportunity for the money that you borrowed. Paying yourself back could take longer than expected. You will also incur fees.

Intermediate-Term Needs: Down Payment, College, Miscellaneous Needs

Your intermediate savings goals depend on lifestyle choices. Although these savings goals are important, they should come after establishing an emergency fund and making regular contributions toward your retirement savings. Having an adequate emergency fund and being on track for retirement should be your top priorities.

For intermediate-term needs, I recommend that you focus on one need or goal at a time. To get to that goal, some investors save a **fixed percentage** of their income, such as 10 percent or 15 percent. This strategy is appealing because it is simple to follow. A fixed percentage gives you the flexibility to save more if your income goes up and save less in a down year. This flexibility also makes it easier to stick with your savings plan. Another example of working toward a savings goal could be, "I want to save between $X and $Y over the next three years." This is a good plan if you are saving for something specific, such as a down payment. Whatever method you use, the important advice here is to develop a plan.

To develop a college savings goal, a friend and her husband analyzed the costs associated with a range of different college options— large public in-state universities, large public out-of-state universities, and small private colleges. They established a 529 plan and set a goal to save more than three years' worth of tuition and expenses for a midpriced option. Remember that money in 529 plans can be used only for qualified expenses, such as tuition, room, and board.

How to Get There: Assumptions for Returns and Growing Your Savings

As you think about how much money you need to meet your savings goals, consider the expected returns for your investment portfolio over the long run. Given volatility in the markets, setting a fixed investment return goal for each year is unrealistic; trying to achieve a certain average return or range of returns over a period of years is more realistic.

No one can predict how investments or the financial markets will perform in a given year or over a long-term horizon. But even though planning for the future involves uncertainty, you need to make some assumptions about growth in your investments to gauge your progress toward attaining your goals.

Simple Calculations to Estimate Growth

There are some helpful rules to consider—ways to compute how quickly investments can grow:

The Rule of 72 calculates how long it takes an investor to double his or her money. As an illustration, assuming an investment generates a return of 7 percent, the number of years to double your investment is 72/7, or a little over ten years.

This is similar to the **Rule of 7s**, according to which it takes ten years to double your money if you earn 7 percent. An investment with a higher return, such as 10 percent, would take only seven years to double your money.

What Annual Return Should You Use to Plan?

As you consider long-term return assumptions, look at the market history for a diversified portfolio of investments. A good rule of thumb is a 6 to 7 percent average return over your planning horizon—whether it is ten, twenty, or thirty years or more. As you think about long-term growth in your assets, don't forget to consider the impact of fees and taxes.

Some industry professionals have commented that individuals can assume long-term investment returns of as much as 10 percent. In my opinion, that is high. It is true that the **compounded annual return**, or **CAGR**, for the S&P 500 since 1970 is approximately 11 percent. A blended portfolio of 60 percent allocated to the S&P 500 and 40 percent allocated to the Barclays US Aggregate Bond Index would have generated a compounded annual return of 10 percent since 1976, which is the first year that the Barclays Index was available.

The compounded annual returns for the markets have come down over the past four decades, as illustrated by table 9.3. I believe this trend is due in part to increased correlation across markets. In addition, interest rates in recent years have been at artificially low levels due to central bank policies. Although financial market returns have come down, the standard deviation, or volatility, within the market is still fairly high. In more recent periods—looking at the past ten years or the past twenty years—compounded annual returns have been in the 6 to 8 percent range, depending on the time frame and mix within a portfolio.

Remember that risk and return go together. Investors can take more risk and look for higher returns when they have a long time horizon. You should take less risk as important milestones, such as kids starting college or beginning your retirement, loom on the horizon. As you get closer to withdrawing money to meet your needs, invest very conservatively in order to preserve your assets.

TABLE 9.3. Long-term returns for equity and bond benchmarks.

Year	S&P 500 Total Return	Barclays US Aggregate Bond Index	Balanced: 60% Equity/40% Bond
1976	23.8%	15.6%	20.5%
1977	-7.2%	3.0%	-3.1%
1978	6.6%	1.4%	4.5%
1979	18.4%	1.9%	11.8%
1980	32.5%	2.7%	20.6%
1981	-4.9%	6.3%	-0.4%
1982	21.6%	32.6%	26.0%
1983	22.6%	8.4%	16.9%
1984	6.3%	15.2%	9.8%
1985	31.7%	22.1%	27.9%
1986	18.7%	15.3%	17.3%
1987	5.3%	2.8%	4.3%
1988	16.6%	7.9%	13.1%
1989	31.7%	14.5%	24.8%
1990	-3.1%	9.0%	1.7%
1991	30.5%	16.0%	24.7%
1992	7.6%	7.4%	7.5%
1993	10.1%	9.8%	9.9%
1994	1.3%	-2.9%	-0.4%
1995	37.6%	18.5%	29.9%
1996	23.0%	3.6%	15.2%
1997	33.4%	9.7%	23.9%
1998	28.6%	8.7%	20.6%
1999	21.0%	-0.8%	12.3%
2000	-9.1%	11.6%	-0.8%
2001	-11.9%	8.4%	-3.8%
2002	-22.1%	10.3%	-9.2%
2003	28.7%	4.1%	18.8%
2004	10.9%	4.3%	8.3%
2005	4.9%	2.4%	3.9%
2006	15.8%	4.3%	11.2%
2007	5.5%	7.0%	6.1%
2008	-37.0%	5.2%	-20.1%
2009	26.5%	5.9%	18.2%
2010	15.1%	6.5%	11.7%
2011	2.1%	7.8%	4.4%
2012	16.0%	4.2%	11.3%
2013	32.4%	-2.0%	18.6%
2014	13.7%	6.0%	10.6%
2015	1.4%	0.6%	1.0%
2016	12.0%	2.7%	8.2%
2017	21.8%	3.5%	14.5%

(continued)

TABLE 9.3. Long-term returns for equity and bond benchmarks *(continued).*

1976–2017	S&P 500 Total Return	Barclays US Aggregate Bond Index	Balanced: 60% Equity/40% Bond
High	37.6%	32.6%	29.9%
Low	-37.0%	-2.9%	-20.1%
CAGR	11.6%	7.5%	10.3%
Median	15.4%	6.4%	11.2%
Std. Dev.	16.1%	6.8%	10.6%

1998–2017	S&P 500 Total Return	Barclays US Aggregate Bond Index	Balanced: 60% Equity/40% Bond
High	32.4%	11.6%	20.6%
Low	-37.0%	-2.0%	-20.1%
CAGR	7.2%	5.0%	6.8%
Median	12.8%	4.8%	9.4%
Std. Dev.	17.9%	3.6%	10.2%

2008–2017	S&P 500 Total Return	Barclays US Aggregate Bond Index	Balanced: 60% Equity/40% Bond
High	32.4%	7.8%	18.6%
Low	-37.0%	-2.0%	-20.1%
CAGR	8.5%	4.0%	7.3%
Median	14.4%	4.7%	10.9%
Std. Dev.	19.3%	3.0%	11.3%

One More Goal: Investing in Others

In addition to developing your savings goals, consider having a family giving policy or charitable mission statement. Prioritize the causes you wish to support financially.

Evaluate donations the same way that you analyze investments. Ask yourself where your donations will have the biggest impact. To ensure that your donation dollars will do the most good possible, look for organizations that use resources efficiently and effectively. Analyze the percentage of donations to an organization that are used to cover administrative and fundraising expenses. If you donate to organizations that spend a low percentage of donations on these expenses, your donations will go further and can have a greater impact. The percentage of donations spent on administration and fundraising should be available in a charity's literature. You can visit Charity Navigator at www.charitynavigator.org and look up a charity. The Better Business Bureau also rates charities.

Each year, I keep a list of donations in Excel. My husband and I prioritize our causes and like to compare giving year-to-year, especially as the year-end approaches. Planning together also helps us to decide whether we can use appreciated securities for donations.

CHAPTER 10

Evaluate Your Investing Choices: What Options Do You Have?

Now that you have determined your saving goals, it is time to think about how to achieve those goals. Your considerations are not just about how much you will need, but also about the types of investments that will help you get there. Figuring out how much money to invest in each asset class is not a one-time exercise. Rather, it is a process that you must revisit from time to time.

To determine the most appropriate way to invest your money, begin by considering your time horizon. The longer you have until retirement or other milestones, such as paying college tuition, the greater the allocation you can have in higher-risk, higher-return assets, such as equities. The shorter the time horizon until you need to meet an obligation, such as paying tuition or making retirement withdrawals, the greater the allocation should be to more conservative investments, such as money market funds.

Think about factors that affect your long-term profile, such as the variability of your earnings, chronic health issues, or your dependents. Consider your profession and industry with respect to your ideal allocation, and make investment choices based on that information. For example, if you work in real estate, don't add to your industry exposure by investing in a lot of real estate investment trusts, or REITs. If your job is in a cyclical industry, don't invest in cyclical stocks. If your compensation is variable, take on less risk. If you have a change in your risk profile—you become a parent, your family goes from two incomes to one, you become divorced or widowed—adjust your allocations. The higher the risk in your life, the lower the risk in your investments should be.

Asset Allocation

There are two types of asset allocations. A **strategic allocation** is based on your individual needs and risk tolerance. Online asset allocation tools are available at Morningstar, Yahoo Finance, and several other financial websites. The most common allocation is 60 percent equity and 40 percent bonds. This is also called a **traditional balanced allocation**. You can use the traditional balanced allocation as a starting point and then adjust your allocation, given your specific needs. Another rule of thumb suggests that you take your age and subtract it from 100, which will tell you the percent of assets that you should have in stock, or equity. If you are 45 years old, this rule suggests that you have 100 minus 45, or 55 percent of your assets in stocks.

. . . .

A widowed relative lived in a home that was paid for, and she had more than sufficient retirement funds to meet her day-to-day needs. She also had a chronic health condition that required expensive medication. The biggest risk she faced was losing her health insurance and prescription drug coverage. She needed to consider the rising cost of health care and her expensive medication as she determined her asset allocation. She decided that she needed a higher allocation to stocks compared with other people her age.

. . . .

Your asset allocation grid shows your current asset allocation and will help you determine what changes you could make to get closer to your strategic allocation. Remember that making changes late in the year can have negative tax consequences. Making changes early in the year gives you time to offset gains with losses.

The other type of allocation is a **tactical allocation**. A tactical allocation is more opportunistic and depends on current market conditions. You can use a tactical allocation to adjust the strategic allocation. For example, you can use a tactical allocation to reduce the amount of money in asset classes that have appreciated considerably and are less attractively valued, and add to asset classes that have underperformed or are more attractively valued. In this case, recall the adage that it is prudent to buy low and sell high.

A Note on Exit Strategies

As you think about how to allocate your assets, focus on a long-term time horizon. At the same time, however, you also need an exit strategy—or a **sell discipline**—for every investment.

In addition to selling an investment that has become significantly overvalued, you may come across other situations that could warrant exiting or selling an investment. The declining creditworthiness of a bond issuer, deteriorating company operating performance, or a significant issue with a company's management could all be reasons to sell or exit an investment. For mutual funds, it might be time

> ## Catch a Falling Knife
>
> There is a difference between buying a stock that is misunderstood or out of favor and buying a stock that is declining in value for a valid reason. For example, if there is evidence of fraud or accounting irregularities, the stock will likely continue to drop. Even though the valuation may be attractive, the value of the stock, like a knife, could keep falling. Whether it is a bad investment or an actual knife, catching it could be very painful.

to sell or redeem the funds if the manager has strayed from his or her mandate. For example, if a value manager starts buying high-growth stocks with high price/earnings multiples, he or she is not sticking with the mandate to invest in value stocks. It may be appropriate to redeem a mutual fund if its performance lags behind peers for several periods.

Never fall in love with an investment. Try to assess each investment objectively. If you don't exit when your exit strategy calls for it, your investment performance will suffer. Recognize when it is time to move on.

CHAPTER 11

Consider Methods: Who Will Do the Investing?

ONCE YOU DETERMINE your ideal asset allocation, you need to figure out if you want to invest on your own or if you will work with a professional.

Going Solo

If you prefer to invest on your own, you can set up an account with one of the large, retail-oriented brokerage firms, such as Schwab, Fidelity, or TD Ameritrade. Invest most of your assets through the same firm to simplify the reporting process. Consolidated reports are especially helpful at tax time. In addition, you will have to consult fewer websites. For diversification, you can invest in a fund or two on your own outside of your brokerage account.

In recent years, there has been a rise in automated investment services, or "robo advisers." These firms provide online wealth management tools using technology, rather than human interaction. The companies begin by surveying clients to determine risk tolerance and then use algorithms to allocate money across various ETFs. Compared with a traditional broker or adviser relationship, these services cost less. They also offer convenience, because most companies rebalance accounts automatically. They do not, however, offer advice or financial planning. If you choose to invest with an automated investment service, make sure that you understand what is in your portfolio. Remember that investing should not be a "set it and forget it" exercise.

Working with a Professional

If you decide to work with an investment professional, the first step is to figure out what type of adviser you want to work with. Brokerage firms are sometimes called broker-dealers. The firm and the individual brokers are regulated as salespeople by the Securities Exchange Act of 1934.

A **registered investment adviser**, or **RIA**, and the firm's professionals working with clients are regulated as financial advisers, rather than as salespeople. RIAs are regulated under the Investment Advisers Act of 1940. For a firm to become a registered investment adviser, the firm must register with the Securities and Exchange Commission, or SEC, or with the state regulatory agency, depending on how much money is managed.

There are a couple of key distinctions between brokers and advisers:

* When making decisions for clients, brokers must use a **suitability standard**. To meet a suitability standard, a broker must consider whether an investment *is suitable* for a client. In other words, the broker must take into account whether an investment is appropriate, given an investor's age, financial situation, and risk tolerance.

- RIAs are fiduciaries and, therefore have a fiduciary duty, or are held to a **fiduciary standard**. To adhere to a fiduciary standard, an adviser must consider whether an investment *is in the best interest* of a client. A fiduciary standard is a higher standard than a suitability standard. A fiduciary standard covers the entire professional relationship and addresses issues such as potential conflicts of interest, advice on asset allocation, and fees and expenses involved. Both the RIA firm and the person associated with it must adhere to a fiduciary standard.

Anyone can use the term "adviser," and some brokers or financial planners offer investment advice relating to retirement and college planning. An investment professional who gives advice is not necessarily a fiduciary who must meet the fiduciary standard.

Professional Credentials

Financial professionals may possess a variety of different licenses, certifications, and designations.

Brokers need a license, or need to be registered representatives, to sell securities. To become a registered representative, brokers must pass the General Securities Representative Exam, or Series 7, and adhere to securities regulations. The Series 7 covers federal securities regulations. Brokers must also pass the Uniform Securities Agent State Law Examination, or Series 63, which covers securities regulations for their state.

The Uniform Investment Adviser Law Examination, or Series 65, may be taken by professionals who give fee-based investment advice. It is not, however, a requirement for giving investment advice. Moreover, the Series 65 is not a license to sell securities. Just as not all professionals giving investment advice work for

RIAs, not all professionals giving investment advice have passed the Series 65 exam.

Licenses indicate that a broker or adviser has met regulatory requirements. Designations or certifications are usually an indication that a broker or an adviser has fulfilled a certain level of educational and professional experience requirements. The list of designations for financial professionals is extensive and can be confusing.

The prestige of designations and their usefulness to clients varies considerably. The Financial Industry Regulatory Authority, or FINRA, has a designation lookup feature on its website: www.finra.org/Investors/ToolsCalculators/ProfessionalDesignations/DesignationsListing. FINRA does not endorse or recommend any of these designations. The tool is very helpful, especially because you can compare different credentials side by side.

As you consider a broker or adviser's credentials, look up what is required to achieve and maintain the various designations. If you need help with retirement planning, what are the prerequisites for becoming a Certified Retirement Financial Advisor (CRFA), a Chartered Retirement Planning Counselor (CRPC), or a Personal Retirement Planning Specialist (PRPS)? If you are looking for advice on estate issues, which professionals are required to complete the most continuing education: an Accredited Estate Planner (AEP), a Certified Estate Planner (CEP), or a Chartered Estate Planning Practitioner (CEPP)?

In my opinion, the most relevant credentials involve an extensive study program, challenging exams, work experience requirements, a code of ethics, and continuing education. Here are some examples:

- A **Certified Public Accountant**, or CPA, is an essential credential for an accountant. Some CPAs manage money after obtaining the Personal Financial Specialist designation.

- The **Certified Financial Planner**™, or CFP®, certification indicates an expertise in financial planning. The certification is designated for fee-based professionals who provide a holistic evaluation of a financial profile and develop a financial plan. Some are also registered investment advisers, or RIAs, and manage clients' money for a fee.
- Professionals who complete the CFA program, which requires extensive study of various investment management topics, earn the **Chartered Financial Analyst**® credential. Many portfolio managers hold this designation.

If you decide to work with a broker or adviser, ask for referrals from family and friends. Make sure that your family and friends have worked with the broker or adviser professionally. Some may know a broker or adviser socially, but it is important that referrals come from professional experience.

You can visit regulatory websites to see if any clients have registered a complaint about a particular professional. FINRA Broker Check (www.finra.org/Investors/ToolsCalculators/BrokerCheck/) is a helpful source. Check with your state regulator at the North American Securities Administrator Association, or NASAA, at www.nasaa.org/about-us/contact-us/contact-your-regulator/. The SEC adviser search (www.adviserinfo.sec.gov/IAPD/Content/Search/iapd_Search.aspx) is another good resource to consult. Check a firm's SEC Form ADV Part 2, which has a lot of information about the firm, including how much money is managed and the fee structure. The form is available on the SEC's website. The firm also can provide a copy.

Ask Questions

When you meet with a prospective broker or adviser, you need to cover certain topics. Evaluate candidates in terms of both their expertise and their interpersonal skills.

What can you tell me about your background and your practice? Ask the adviser for a basic overview of his or her practice. What is the adviser's educational and professional background? Is the adviser a broker or a fiduciary? How does the adviser get paid? What fees does he or she charge clients? What types of investments and products does the adviser use for clients' portfolios?

There is a distinction between funds and investment products from outside sources and funds and investment products from in-house, or proprietary, sources. **Proprietary products** are mutual funds or other investment funds that are managed and distributed by a broker or adviser's firm. A broker or adviser offering only proprietary products should be a concern because incentives to use the firm's products can create a conflict of interest. Are those proprietary products in your best interest? Are investment products offered by other firms a better fit for your particular needs? Some firms offer an **open architecture** platform, which means that the firm uses products from a number of vendors. In this case, make sure the vendors are truly independent and are not related, or affiliated, firms. For outside vendors, ask about compensation and revenue-sharing arrangements.

As you discuss the types of products offered, keep in mind that not all investment products are considered securities. For example, stocks, bonds, and options are securities, but fixed annuities are not—they are insurance products. The distinction is important in terms of how each is regulated and who may be able to help investors if things go wrong. The Securities and Exchange Commission cannot become involved if the investment is not a security.

Are the accounts discretionary or nondiscretionary? **Discretionary** means that the adviser can make investment decisions without consulting you first. With a **nondiscretionary** account, the broker or adviser must check with you before buying or selling anything in the account. A discretionary account involves a contractual relationship. Whether you should choose a discretionary account depends on how well you know and trust the investment professional.

If you decide to work with a professional, don't forget to consider diversification and concentration. You should not have all your investments managed by one person or one firm. Invest in some stocks, bonds, or funds outside of your broker or adviser relationship. Make sure to inform your adviser about the other investments, so there are no redundancies or concentration issues. This is especially important if your broker or adviser has discretion over your account.

What is the arrangement for custody? A registered investment adviser, or RIA, can act as custodian, but is subject to surprise verifications or audits. A large, established third-party custodian may be a safer option than having a smaller RIA have custody of your assets. Large brokerage firms and global banks, such as Citibank, State Street, and Schwab, are examples of custodians. On a day-to-day basis, excellent bookkeeping and reporting are essential not only for the safety of your assets but also for tax purposes. The large custodians usually have the most up-to-date systems.

How effectively does the broker or adviser explain things? Interpersonal skills are critical. In addition to having a similar investment philosophy, do you and the investment professional communicate well? The investment professional should explain investment options in plain English. To make sure that you really understand the features of an investment and how it works, try explaining the investment, its benefits, and its risks to another person.

Although it is essential that your broker or adviser have good interpersonal skills, you must keep the relationship professional. Confirm expectations and be clear that you will move your account if the manager does not do what you have requested. Everything—including any discussion of fees—should be in writing.

What is the succession plan? Who will take over if something happens to your broker or adviser or if he or she retires? Many investment professionals work in teams. You need to ensure that you are comfortable with the other team members.

If the Relationship Does Not Work

When you are searching for an investment professional, the goal should be to find the right fit for the long run. If your broker or adviser does not meet agreed-upon objectives, be prepared to end the relationship. Just as you need to maintain a sell discipline for your investments, there are legitimate reasons to fire an investment professional. If fees increase significantly, if the strategy changes without your consent, if the adviser is not responsive to your needs, or if performance consistently falls short of expectations, it makes sense to move on.

If you decide to switch to a professional at a different firm, monitor the transfer of assets very closely. The original brokerage firm will not necessarily make it easy for the new adviser or broker. In particular, make sure that cost basis information is complete. Incomplete or inaccurate information is a hassle at tax time and could result in unanticipated capital gains. Confirm that all information is complete before the new adviser starts making any changes to the portfolio. The new broker or adviser may want to sell holdings rather than have his or her performance measured based on a legacy portfolio. If your original broker or adviser manages your IRA, make sure to transfer the assets directly into another retirement account. You want to avoid an unplanned-for distribution of retirement assets. An unintended retirement account distribution could generate penalties and taxes.

CHAPTER 12

Evaluate Metrics for Potential Investments: Which Investments Are Best?

A s YOU DETERMINE which funds to invest in or which broker or adviser to hire, there are some important metrics to consider. Performance is a key consideration; various ways to analyze the performance of a prospective investment or investment professional are covered in this chapter. There are also other metrics to consider that will help you determine the quality and risks associated with different investment options.

Performance Metrics

As you evaluate investment options, start with an analysis of investment performance. Whether you are looking at a fund or at the track record of a financial professional, always consider total return, or capital appreciation plus interest or dividends. You should also evaluate advisers after fees, or on a net basis. If performance is presented before fees, or on a gross basis, adjust the performance by subtracting the fee percentage. You should also evaluate performance over different time horizons, such as for one-, three-, and five-year periods and since inception, or the beginning, of the fund. For separately managed accounts, a broker or adviser can provide investment performance information on the **composite**, or aggregation of all accounts using the same investment strategy. Performance metrics should adhere to the Global Investment Performance Standards, or GIPS, from the CFA Institute.

Benchmarks

Whether you invest on your own or work with a professional, you should consider benchmarks. **Benchmarks** show how a fund or a manager performed relative to a market index. Determine the most appropriate benchmark for a specific fund or a broker or adviser's investment strategy. The Dow Jones industrial average is often quoted in the financial press, but that index consists of only thirty stocks.

The S&P 500 is the most common benchmark for equity funds or portfolios. It is actually a large-cap stock index, but it is the main benchmark for stock funds and separate accounts. Active equity managers should justify their performance—and their fee—relative to the S&P 500 because index funds based on that index are a low-cost alternative to active management.

Compare a fund's or a manager's performance with more specialized indexes if appropriate. If you are considering a small-cap manager or a small-cap mutual fund, you should also compare the performance of a small-cap manager or small-cap mutual fund to the Russell 2000 Index. The MSCI EAFE is a common benchmark for international stocks or funds. The Barclays US Aggregate Bond Index is the most widely used benchmark for bonds.

Peer Group Performance

In addition to evaluating funds or managers relative to a benchmark, consider how well the fund or manager performs relative to its peer group or category. Categories represent a more specialized subsection of a broader asset class. Examples include large-cap value equity, small-cap growth equity, and high-yield bonds. Morningstar is a good source for category performance.

For funds, don't simply choose the highest ranking among its peers. Being the top performer in a category is hard to sustain. Instead look for consistently good performance, a fund manager that remains in the top 50 percent of the category, and, perhaps most important, a manager that does relatively better on the downside. Good relative performance in down markets is essential.

Performance in Down Markets

Whether you choose to work with a broker or adviser or choose your own investments and funds, good relative performance when times are tough is essential for the long-term growth of your investments. When evaluating investment or financial professionals, focus on the performance record during a period of market turmoil, such as in 2008, when the S&P 500 declined 37 percent. Look at how a prospective manager or fund fared during a turbulent time.

In addition to looking at challenging periods, analyze upside and downside capture for an investment, whether it is a fund or a portfolio managed by your broker or adviser. For time periods with positive market returns, **upside capture** illustrates how much a fund or portfolio gained relative to the positive performance of the benchmark or index. For periods with negative market returns, **downside capture** looks at how much the investment participated in the downside performance of the benchmark or index. If capture is less than 100 percent, the investment did not rise (upside) or fall (downside) as much as the benchmark or index. If capture is more than 100 percent, the investment rose more than (upside) or fell more than (downside) the benchmark or index. Ideally, upside capture should exceed downside capture. If it does not, you would be taking on too much risk for the expected return.

Table 12.1 illustrates the importance of having less downside capture. This example assumes a loss of 37 percent in year 1, comparable to the market decline in 2008. This was the worst annual decline in the S&P 500 during my lifetime. Another noteworthy market decline occurred in the mid-1970s. In 1973 and 1974, losses totaled 37 percent over the two-year period. As illustrated in table 12.2, having less downside capture allows you to recover losses much faster.

TABLE 12.1. Impact of downside capture.

Example of full downside capture—37 percent decline

Year	Return	Ending balance	Year	Return	Ending balance
0		$1,000	0		$1,000
1	-37.0%	$630	1	-37.0%	$630
2	7.0%	$674	2	5.0%	$662
3	7.0%	$721	3	5.0%	$695
4	7.0%	$772	4	5.0%	$729
5	7.0%	$826	5	5.0%	$766
6	7.0%	$884	6	5.0%	$804
7	7.0%	$945	7	5.0%	$844
8	7.0%	**$1,012**	8	5.0%	$886
9	7.0%	$1,082	9	5.0%	$931
10	7.0%	$1,158	10	5.0%	$977
11	7.0%	$1,239	11	5.0%	**$1,026**

TABLE 12.2. Impact of downside capture.

Example of less downside capture—27 percent decline

Year	Return	Ending balance	Year	Return	Ending balance
0		$1,000	0		$1,000
1	-27.0%	$730	1	-27.0%	$730
2	7.0%	$781	2	5.0%	$767
3	7.0%	$836	3	5.0%	$805
4	7.0%	$894	4	5.0%	$845
5	7.0%	$957	5	5.0%	$887
6	7.0%	**$1,024**	6	5.0%	$932
7	7.0%	$1,096	7	5.0%	$978
8	7.0%	$1,172	8	5.0%	**$1,027**
9	7.0%	$1,254	9	5.0%	$1,079

Among investors, there is a lot of discussion regarding the merits of active investing versus passive investing, such as using a market-based index fund. Active managers might find it difficult to beat a market index, especially in momentum or hot markets. But having less downside capture is a beneficial attribute of some active managers. Market-based index funds have 100 percent downside capture. An active manager could construct a portfolio that performs relatively better on the downside, however, and the fund would have less than 100 percent downside capture.

Other Metrics and Factors

In addition to performance, several other metrics are useful as you consider investment options. Most metrics can be used for an investable asset, a fund, or a separate account. Compare all metrics with those for the appropriate benchmark indices and with the peer group.

Valuation Metrics

For equities or equity funds, the key valuation metrics are:

- The price/earnings ratio based on prospective earnings
- Long-term earnings growth
- The price/earnings-to-growth, or PEG, ratio
- The price/book value ratio
- The dividend yield

Risk Metrics

Risk is measured by beta, standard deviation, or the amount of leverage, or debt, on a company's balance sheet. Beta and standard deviation measure the volatility of returns. Leverage is usually measured by the debt/equity ratio or the debt/capitalization ratio. For the debt/capitalization ratio, capitalization refers to a company's entire capital structure and includes both equity and debt. It is not the market capitalization of the company. Substantial leverage, or debt, has an impact on a company's ability to manage through tough times. Look at the weighted average beta, standard deviation, and leverage of a portfolio or fund as an indication of the aggregate risk associated with the underlying holdings.

Keep in mind that risk measures can change over time. For bonds and bond funds, consider credit rating and duration. Monitor bond risk metrics periodically because they can change over time.

Manager Tenure

Manager tenure, or the number of years that a manager has been in charge of a fund or managing separate accounts, is meaningful. There should be consistency in the person or team managing your money. Sometimes a fund is subadvised by a team of portfolio managers from another asset management firm. This is not cause for concern. A team of portfolio managers may have been chosen to subadvise a fund because they have expertise not present in a particular asset management firm. Remember that you are analyzing the fund, its risk, its performance, and the experience and track record of the portfolio managers. Whether they work for the asset management firm offering the fund or are subadvising the fund is not as important.

Additional Metrics

For funds, the total assets under management, or AUM, and the number of holdings are important. Mutual funds with a substantial number of holdings may not be able to perform better than the overall market. A stock fund with 350 holdings will likely perform more like the S&P 500 Index—with 500 holdings—than a fund with only 35 holdings. Each of those 35 holdings has more of an impact on performance than each of the 350 holdings in the other fund. The portfolio with 350 holdings also has a higher fee than an index fund. The same is true for bonds. For broad exposure to the bond market, investing in the Barclays US Aggregate Bond Index may be the best option. Remember that if the assets under management are large, it may be hard for a portfolio manager to buy and sell holdings without moving the market.

There are other characteristics to consider:

- Look at fees compared with the average for the asset class or what other brokers or advisers are charging for a separate account.
- High portfolio turnover can lead to increased transaction costs and short-term capital gains.
- For stock funds, look at the market capitalization of the underlying holdings in the portfolio. A small-cap fund may actually contain a lot of midcap stocks.
- Identify cross holdings, or stocks or bonds that are also in other investments that you already own. You may have more concentration than you realize.

CHAPTER 13

Monitor Your Investments: How Are You Doing?

ANAGING YOUR financial life is not a "set it and forget it" exercise. Once you have made your investing decisions and implemented your investment program, you need to monitor it on an ongoing basis.

Keep up with the financial news by reading periodicals such as the *Wall Street Journal*. There are many sources of financial news in print, online, and on television. Keeping up to date is essential as you monitor your investments.

Performance

Look at the performance of your investments regularly but not daily. Daily market fluctuations can cause you undue stress. If you reinvest dividends and interest and do not add to or withdraw money from a separate account or fund, use the following formula to determine the total return percentage after fees, or on a net basis:

(Ending account balance/beginning account balance) −1

Subtracting 1 from the ratio of the ending balance over the beginning balance will give you a decimal. Then convert the decimal to a percentage. For example 0.10 equals 10 percent. If you do not reinvest dividends or interest or add to or withdraw money from the account or fund, the performance calculation is more complex. The manager or mutual fund can provide you the figures for net performance.

You should also evaluate how you are doing relative to your benchmarks. Benchmarks are helpful when monitoring individual funds or separate accounts. You can use a blended benchmark to assess the performance of a diversified pool or even your asset allocation. If your asset allocation contains 60 percent stocks and 40 percent bonds, for example, use a blended benchmark of 60 percent of the performance of the S&P 500 and 40 percent of the Barclays US Aggregate Bond Index.

As your needs change, you may require a different asset allocation. If your asset allocation changes, so should your benchmarks. If you are working with a financial professional and he or she changes a benchmark without a good reason, it is a red flag. Some brokers or advisors may try to change a benchmark if the adviser is not performing well relative to originally agreed-upon benchmarks.

Look for Overlap Across Your Investments

From time to time, check to see if there is overlap or redundancy across your investments. As portfolio managers make changes to the funds, some holdings could pop up in more than one of your investments. Morningstar and other online resources can provide information on the overlap in different mutual funds.

Rebalance

Revisit and update your asset allocation grid periodically. The returns for your various investments will vary. Some investments will increase in value more than others. As a result, the amount of assets in some asset classes will grow more than others. Over time, your current asset allocation will move away from your original strategic allocation.

You may have to rebalance, or reallocate, your portfolio on occasion. Prioritize your next investment by determining what you should buy or sell. Look at your needs and how your investments have performed, and revisit your sell discipline. You may buy more shares of stock or of a fund, or add to a position. You may decide to sell some of your holdings or trim a position.

Portfolio managers maintain a **watch list** of investments that they have analyzed and would like to buy but that may be too expensive. You can do this too. Look for opportunities to invest in stocks that you have monitored and that have become more attractively valued.

When you rebalance, you can trim positions or asset classes that have appreciated and add to positions or asset classes that have not appreciated and are more attractively valued. But don't rebalance with every minor diversion from your asset allocation targets. Rebalancing can result in transaction costs. You should not rebalance at the end of the year, because you might generate a taxable gain. Earlier in the year, there is time to offset a gain with a capital loss.

Going Forward

Not only is it important to monitor your investments, you also need to take a step back from time to time and reevaluate your financial profile and your individual needs. As you probably have realized by now, managing your financial life is not a linear process. It is an ongoing, circular process. You don't finish the task and set it aside. Rather, you need to revisit the steps outlined in this book.

Maintain your system and reevaluate your financial profile and needs. Stay up to date with your investments and what is going on in the financial world. Managing your financial life is a dynamic process, not a static one.

Just like managing your health or your home, managing your financial life requires an investment of your time as well as your money. If you make this process part of your routine, you can relax, knowing that you are indeed in control of your financial life.

Notes

1. Jonathan Vespa, Jamie M. Lewis, and Rose M. Kreider, "America's Families and Living Arrangements: Population Characteristics"(August 2013), page 5; Bureau of the Census for the Bureau of Labor Statistics, "Current Population Survey: 2017 Annual Social and Economic (ASEC) Supplement" (Washington, DC: US Census, 2017), https://www2.census.gov/programs-surveys/cps/techdocs/cpsmar17.pdf.

2. US Census Bureau, Decennial Census (1960); and "Current Population Survey."

3. "Current Population Survey."

4. National Center for Health Statistics, "Health, United States, 2016" (Washington, DC: Centers for Disease Control, 2016), https://www.cdc.gov/nchs/hus/contents2016.htm#015.

5. Rose M. Kreider and Renee Ellis, "Number, Timing, and Duration of Marriages and Divorces: 2009" (Washington, DC: US Census Bureau, 2011).

6. "Trends in the Expenses and Fees of Funds, 2016," ICI Research Perspective 22, no. 3 (May 2017).

Index

Page numbers in italics refer to tables and figures. Page numbers in boldface denote terms printed in boldface in the book.

About the Author

Nancy Doyle is the founder of The Doyle Group, LLC; she has thirty years' experience in wealth management, investments, finance, and consulting. She is a graduate of Georgetown University, received her MBA from University of Michigan's Ross School of Business, and holds the Chartered Financial Analyst® (CFA®) designation. In addition to her passion for financial literacy and organization, she is active in her community. Ms. Doyle, her husband, and their two children live near Chicago.

CPSIA information can be obtained
at www.ICGtesting.com
Printed in the USA
FFOW03n2303050318
45459413-46184FF